Rainforests

WILDSIDE

Paul Appleby

Conserving animals and plants in a changing world

BBC BOOKS

Published by BBC Books,
a division of BBC Enterprises Limited,
Woodlands, 80 Wood Lane, London W12 0TT

First published 1992

© Paul Appleby 1992

ISBN 0 563 36165 4

Designed by Neville Graham

Printed in Great Britain by
Butler & Tanner Ltd, Frome and London

Contents

The richest place on Earth 4
Vanishing forest – the past 6
Vanishing forest – the future? .. 8
Deep in the forest 10
The global greenhouse 12
Breaking the cycle 14
Reaching for the sky 16
Plants in mid-air 18
Living leather 20
Keeping warm? 22
Paradise lost? 24
The butterfly trade 26
Big rhinos, small insects 28
Old men of the forest 30
A future in the trees? 32
Forests under the sea 34
The endangered island 36
Jungle action 38
A watery wilderness 40
Damming the rivers 42
Giants in danger 44
Lying low 46
Into the darkness 48
An eagle's domain 50
Fleeing the fires 52
Using the forest 54
Green deserts 56
Eating the rainforest 58
Gone for ever? 60
Save the rainforest! 62
Useful addresses 63
Index 64

About this book

THE RAINFOREST is the most important natural habitat on Earth. Animals of every shape and size live there: tiny insects, tree-frogs, large rhinos, birds of all the colours of the rainbow, deadly snakes, fish, big cats like the secretive jaguar. Millions of plant species make up the forest vegetation, from tall hardwood trees to microscopic water plants. The variety is astonishing.

But the rainforest is also the scene of the largest destruction by man ever known. Burning and felling goes on all the time and every day huge areas disappear for ever. This book looks at how the ecology of the rainforest works and at what happens when we interfere with it. The Wildside approach puts nature first, finding out what the wildlife needs from the forest, and how natural systems are being altered by humans. It looks at the animals and plants of the forest and the problems they are now facing.

Many of the things we use every day come from the forest: wood, cocoa, bananas, beneficial drugs. Once we understand how these products connect us to the rainforest we can see how our everyday lives affect it. Even very small changes in the way we live can make a real difference. This book shows what you can do yourself to help protect wildlife and save the rainforest from further destruction.

The richest place on Earth

The forest mosaic

IMAGINE A VAST, hot, humid green cathedral: its pillars are tree trunks, and its ceiling, over 30 m (100 ft) high, is formed from branches that spread widely, blocking out most of the light. It stretches for thousands of miles, sliced through here and there by rivers. It is a rainforest.

Rainforest is by far the richest habitat on Earth. It covers only 7 per cent of the surface, but contains at least half of the species – in any acre there may be over 150 different plants, including 60 tree species. Living on them is a huge variety of insects, frogs, birds and mammals, all bound together in the rainforest mosaic, feeding on the fruit and leaves and each other.

Above right: Rainforest may stretch for thousands of square kilometres. The combination of warmth and moisture is ideal for plants, so the vegetation is extremely dense.
Right: Rainforest animals are often spectacular. This rufous-breasted hermit hummingbird is hovering in space to drink nectar from a flower.
Below: This is the Rajah Brooke's birdwing, from Malaysia, one of the largest rainforest butterflies.
Below right: Squirrel monkeys live in groups in the Amazon rainforest.

WILDSIDE WATCH

How much wildlife is there around you?
● Take a look at your local park. There may be five or six types of tree, plus other plants – the grass, dandelions, daisies and buttercups, perhaps some shrubs, and a few birds and squirrels.
● But on every tree in a tropical rainforest, there may be up to 150 species of insect, plants growing on the tree itself, and frogs and birds nesting higher up.

Rainforest in danger

THE RAINFOREST is being destroyed on a massive scale, to make money from short-term agriculture and logging, and to provide land for expanding populations. Any profitable trees are taken out, destroying all the others in the process.

The trees bind the soil together, so if they are removed, the soil turns to dust. Replacing the trees with grass is doomed to failure, since the soil is poor and soon becomes choked with weeds. The complex plant and animal mosaic cannot return, but there's always another area to exploit, and the path of destruction moves on.

Above left: Destroying the trees doesn't leave a complete desert, since the ashes contain nutrients and elements that help crops or grasses to grow. But the rich variety of plants and animals has gone, and the soil will soon be exhausted.
Left: Many forest countries simply have too many people. These childen with their crop of bananas live in a village in the rainforest of Cameroon, West Africa.
Below left: Hundreds of years of growth can be reduced to timber in just a few hours. These trees have been taken from the forest of Sarawak, in Borneo.
Below: Once the land has been cleared, what use is it for farming? Replacing trees with cattle is economic nonsense, but even so ranches are common.

WILDSIDE WATCH

The forests are exploited for three things that involve you:
- **Hardwood** – the slow-growing trees produce very dense, strong wood. We should be using other hardwoods instead, such as oak, ash or beech.
- **Crops** – plantations in the forest produce coffee, cocoa, even the gum in chewing gum!
- **Beef** – the forest is felled for cattle pasture, to meet the increased world demand for beef.

Vanishing forest – the past

THE TERM 'RAINFOREST' covers a wide range of different habitats all round the world. They form a band round the Equator between the Tropics, covering about seven per cent of the Earth's surface, and all have an average temperature of over 26°C (80°F) and annual rainfall between 300 and 600 cm (120–240 in).

This combination of warmth and moisture is ideal for plant growth, making the forests a very rich resource for harvesting over the centuries by the forest people. Many forests were untouched until the last century, but since then the demands of the industrial world and the use of machinery have turned a natural harvest into unnatural destruction.

Many countries with rainforest also have a rapidly increasing human population, where the forests are seen as a wilderness ready to be cut down to give landless people a place to live. This is particularly the case in Africa.

Where are the rainforests?

BY FAR THE BIGGEST area of rainforest is the Amazon basin of South America, extending up into Central America. In Africa there are two major areas: the Zairean forest around the Zaire river, stretching into the highlands of Central Africa, and the smaller Guinean forest running along the southern edge of West Africa.

There are also two main areas in South-East Asia, one spreading down the mainland of Malaysia to Indonesia, and the other spreading up from Queensland in Australia to the island of New Guinea.

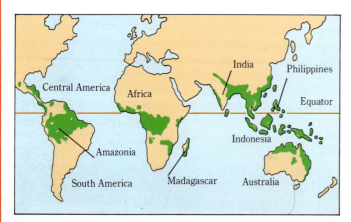

Prehistoric forests

THE EARTH HAS BEEN losing its forest cover naturally for millions of years, as the global climate has become drier. When dinosaurs ruled the earth, over 65 million years ago, there was much more forest and swamp than there is today.

It used to be thought that the huge rainforest areas were the remains of these forests, unchanged for millions of years. But the diversity of animal life suggests another theory, that the forests gradually shrank to form 'islands' of dense vegetation in a grassy savannah. In each island, the creatures evolved in different ways, and later the islands expanded and merged, but with very different species now living side by side. Modern rainforest surveys show that areas just a few kilometres apart have different species of insects or birds doing the same job, because once they may have been on different islands!

Over 100 million years ago, primitive rainforest was home to dinosaurs like this crested hadrosaur which lived on the leaves of ferns and pine trees.

The age of man

TRACING THE EARLY history of man is very difficult, and most evidence is found in the grass savannah of East Africa. But there are traces of early man in the rainforests of Java and Borneo, dating from one million years ago. Our species *homo sapiens* is also found in these areas, from about 40,000 years ago.

The first groups lived as 'hunter-gatherers', eating the nuts, fruits and animals around them, and often living by rivers or estuaries. Plant remains from Thailand show their diet included peas, beans and rice, but it is not clear whether these were gathered or planted.

By 6000 BC the forest dwellers were keeping domestic animals and using pottery, so they almost certainly cleared areas of forest for agriculture. Prehistoric rock paintings show that 6000 years ago, there were forests in Morocco and Algeria. Since then, huge areas of forest have been cleared throughout the world.

There are still hunter-gatherers in the forest. These Yanomami Indians from Brazil are returning from a hunt with an ant-eater for the pot.

The Europeans arrive

IT WAS THE ARRIVAL of European traders in the rainforest regions that turned harvesting into destruction. The first 'cash crop' in South America was sugar. In the Middle Ages, honey satisfied the European demand for sweetness, but the discovery of sugar cane brought the industry to the tropics. In 1530 the Portuguese took over Brazil, destroyed the coastal forest to plant sugar canes, and imported slaves from Africa to work the plantations.

By 1600 the Dutch had started plantations in the Caribbean, where the delicate island wildlife was wiped out – in the lowlands for sugar, in the uplands to provide wood for fuel. Tree-felling was mainly for the dyes in the bark – in fact Brazil is named after a tree called pau-brazil, which gave a very fashionable purple dye. It is now virtually extinct in the wild.

This is the scene at a seventeenth-century sugar-cane crushing mill in the Caribbean. To extract the sugary sap the cane was crushed using water-power, but it was cut by hand. Cane-cutting is very hard work, and most workers were slaves taken from Africa.

WILDSIDE WATCH

There are always lessons in history.
● The earth is always changing, but at a natural rate. The human rate of change is unnatural, demanding food, water and space.
● The human population is increasing very rapidly, mainly in areas that have rainforests of global importance.
● Every Western country demands economic 'growth' – that means more industrial production and more consumption every year, until the earth's resources run dry.
● Every single one of us could make better, more natural use of the earth.

Vanishing forest – the future?

FROM THE SIXTEENTH to the eighteenth centuries, the Europeans built huge empires in the tropics, paving the way for the enormous trade of the British Empire. Coffee, cocoa and sugar then became important tropical crops, with plantations of one species replacing the huge variety of the forest. The tall, straight hardwood trees were also felled for the timber trade.

After the American Civil War, trade with the United States increased and with it the mechanised destruction of the forests. The 1950s saw another great leap up in the use of tropical forests, as the modern consumer society began.

The nineteenth century

THE VICTORIANS saw Africa as the 'Dark Continent' – a forbidding, dangerous place. There was some trade in hardwood with coastal colonies like Nigeria, and in the oilpalm nuts that grew in the deltas of the Niger and Zaire rivers.

But in the nineteenth century the demand for hardwood increased, mainly for use in ship-building. Felling in the colonies was so great that by 1900 the Caribbean forests had been depleted of all major hardwood trees.

Coffee had also become an international crop. In 1830 the former Spanish colonies of Brazil, Colombia and Central America cleared and planted huge areas with coffee bushes, but by 1860 a large area had turned to desert, and the plantations were moved into Amazonia.

The story was the same in West Africa, but here the crop was cacao, a natural plant of the region but grown in plantations of just that one species – a biological desert.

In 1830 the former Spanish colonies of Brazil and Colombia cleared huge areas to plant coffee, using slave labour. The Brazilian state of Sao Paulo was one of these, but by 1860 it had become a desert.

Modern times

AT THE BEGINNING of this century, the cash crops of sugar, coffee and cocoa were joined by a demand for fruit. Huge banana plantations appeared in Central America, but were hit by disease in the 1920s. The only solution was to clear new areas and move the plantations every ten years – leaving a great swathe of destruction. This clearance reduced the coastal forests of the Caribbean islands to a desert, and by 1945 the Ecuadorean forest too was being felled, making Ecuador a world leader in the banana trade.

The timber trade also was mechanised, particularly by the Japanese in South-East Asia. More trees were felled and more destruction accompanied the felling. By 1960 the Philippines' timber trade was starting to fall and the country ended up becoming an importer of timber. The same has happened in Thailand: in 1960 53 per cent of the country was forest, now it's just 29 per cent. Now the rate of destruction is even more alarming – 1.8 per cent of all rainforest is destroyed each year, almost twice as much as in the 1970s.

The future looks bleak. It is quite possible that by the year 2000 the only rainforest left will be in western Amazonia, the Zaire basin, Guyana and New Guinea. This is not just a sad loss of plants and animals. We can only guess at its effect on the world as a whole, on weather patterns or pollution – things that will affect all of us.

Above: Much of the Caribbean rainforest was destroyed for banana plantations. In the West Indies, few islands have harbours, so rafts took the fruit out to the banana boats, where they were loaded by hand.

Left: Before the arrival of hand-held chainsaws, trees were felled by hand. This tree, in the British Honduras, was felled in the 1920s, after several hours of chopping.

Below left: In the 1920s, machines like these arrived in the rainforest. The huge tree-trunks were pulled by steam-driven caterpillar tractors, and cut with power-saws. Now more trees could be felled, but larger areas were destroyed in the process.

WILDSIDE WATCH

There's nothing we can do about the population increase in Brazil, or the international debt of Nigeria, except support positive ideas for change.
● That means supporting the charities that work in these countries, with both wildlife and people.
● But do you like chocolate? In eastern Brazil, 96.5 per cent of the rainforest has been destroyed to provide sugar and cocoa, so eat less chocolate.
● Think about our use of resources. What dictates our spending: need or fashion? Do you always use everything you buy?

Deep in the forest

SUNLIGHT PROVIDES the energy for all the life in the forest. Plants use it directly to make their own food and to grow, herbivorous animals eat the plants, and carnivorous animals eat the herbivores.

Around the Equator, the strong sunlight lasts for 12 hours every day, summer and winter, a brilliant energy-source. To compete for the sunlight, trees grow tall, narrow trunks topped by horizontal branches that catch as much light as possible.

The forest layers

THE DENSEST GROWTH may be 30 m (100 ft) up in the air – in the 'canopy' formed by the branches. Some tree species grow beyond the canopy, standing out like islands in the sea of green. Others will grow into the space below the canopy, where the dim light level forces them to stay as shrubs or straggly vines.

The forest floor gets only one per cent of the light. It's a tangle of undergrowth, tree saplings, creepers and vines. Insects and fungi break down the fallen leaves and wood, releasing the goodness back into the soil.

WILDSIDE WATCH

- Until recently, scientists thought there were about 1.5 million species of animals on earth.
- Research in rainforests finds new species every day – maybe the figure should be 15 million!
- Why not join the Tropical Rainforest Campaign run by the Friends of the Earth (see page 63)?

Super-canopy
The tallest trees in the forest may top 40m (130ft). This is where the eagles nest, and monkeys leap around.

Howler monkeys live in social groups of 8–20 animals, and are the noisiest of all the species, with a large lower jaw adapted as a resonating chamber. They are big monkeys, perfectly adapted for tree life with grasping hands and feet and a prehensile tail. They move quite slowly, ranging several hundred metres a day and eating flowers and leaves.

Canopy
The important thing about rainforest is that the goodness is not in the soil, but in the trees. This means most of the wildlife is over 30m (100ft) off the ground. That includes mammals, snakes and even frogs.

The pools of water that collect around the bromeliad leaves are ideal for tree-frogs to lay their eggs. Later the female will move one or two tadpoles to another pond, carrying them on her back. Tree-frogs have suckers to help them climb around the leaves, and the damp air is ideal for their moist skin.

Understorey
One of the most extraordinary forest animals is the tamandua, a tree-climbing ant-eater from South America. It has a very long pencil-thin tongue for lapping up termites and ants, and climbs with the help of a prehensile tail. Like many rainforest animals tamanduas are nocturnal, with poor eyesight but good hearing, and they live a solitary existence most of the year.

Tree-snakes like the paradise tree-snake from Borneo climb vertical trunks by digging in with their scales. They feed on mammals, birds and insects, and can drop from the trees to the ground, 'flying' by spreading their ribs.

Forest floor
The forest floor is home for a myriad of insects, from tiny ants and termites to huge stick-insects. Army ants swarm across the floor in search of prey.

The cock-of-the-rock birds of South America use the forest floor as an arena for group displays, making rapid jumps from low perches to the ground, fluffing up their feathers and head-bobbing.

The global greenhouse

A GREENHOUSE works very simply. The sunlight passes down through the glass, warms up the ground and the heat is reflected back up. But instead of passing out through the glass, it is reflected back in again, as the panes of glass trap the heat energy from the sunlight. This warms the plants, so their systems work more efficiently and they grow faster.

The Earth's atmosphere is just like the panes of glass, letting the sunlight through, and bouncing the reflected heat back in. When the atmosphere has a high level of carbon dioxide, or some other gases like methane or CFCs, the temperature increase is greater.

How trees breathe

THE WHOLE of life on Earth depends on a simple chemical reaction that happens inside the cells of green plants. The green pigment chlorophyll combines carbon dioxide gas from the air with water drawn up from the ground to produce carbohydrate and oxygen. The reaction builds simple molecules into complex ones, and this requires energy, which is provided by sunlight.

The leaf is a biological factory. Its broad, flat shape is designed to catch the energy of the sun like a solar panel. The underside is porous to allow the gases in and out, and it is connected to the water supply, via the plant's roots.

Since the advent of green plants over 1000 million years ago, the whole of the planet has relied on this simple reaction to produce food, generate oxygen, remove carbon dioxide, and maintain a healthy balance. Now that balance is threatened by man.

Heat reflected back into the atmosphere

Industry
We burn carbon – coal and oil – to produce power in the form of electricity. Power stations and factories give off an enormous amount of carbon dioxide, about 5.6 billion tonnes a year in the industrial areas of Europe, Japan and America. Carbon dioxide is a gas – a litre weighs only two grams – so this is pollution on a massive scale.

Motor vehicles
Cars, motorcycles and lorries, indeed anything that runs on petrol, give off carbon dioxide in their exhaust fumes, adding to the greenhouse effect. The level of carbon dioxide in the air is considerably higher now than it was 150 years ago.

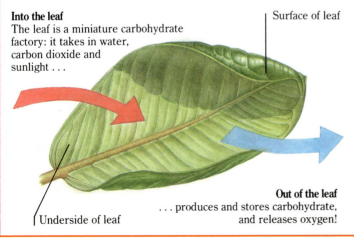

Into the leaf
The leaf is a miniature carbohydrate factory: it takes in water, carbon dioxide and sunlight ...

Surface of leaf

Underside of leaf

Out of the leaf
... produces and stores carbohydrate, and releases oxygen!

Heat trapped by 'greenhouse' gases

Heat from the sun

Forest destruction
When the forests are cut down, they can no longer absorb carbon dioxide. When they are burned, the effect is even worse: it releases more carbon dioxide into the atmosphere, about another 2 billion tonnes per year.

Droughts and floods
If the Earth warms up, there will be more droughts. Flooding is another very serious possibility: the polar ice-caps could begin to melt, raising the sea-level and causing disastrous floods to low-lying areas such as Bangladesh and islands in the Pacific. The United States is spending huge amounts on flood defences, but not on the trees that could solve the problem at its source.

Rainforests
The rainforests are large enough to absorb carbon dioxide and produce oxygen on a global scale: one-third of all the world's oxygen is produced by rainforests. They act as a vital air-conditioning service for the Earth.

WILDSIDE WATCH

We are responsible for most of the greenhouse effect. We use fossil fuels to generate electricity and to power motor vehicles.
● **Use less electricity:** switch off lights and use energy-efficient bulbs.
● **Persuade your family to insulate** your house properly so you need less heating.
● **Use cars less:** walk or cycle whenever you can. A 10 per cent saving would reduce carbon dioxide emissions by millions of tons.
● **We are now very unnatural animals.** How often do you sit in the warm when it's cold outside, or sit in the light when it's dark? These things are part of 'civilised life', but they put the world out of balance.

Breaking the cycle

IMAGINE YOU ARE a plant, in the middle of the forest. In order to breed, you have to get your pollen to a neighbour of the same species, but the problem is that there are so many different plants around that your neighbour is a long way away. Simply casting pollen on the wind is a waste of time: you need an animal to carry it – one that will come to your flowers, then go straight to your nearest neighbour and leave the pollen there. So practically all the plants in the forest need a specific type of animal in order to survive. But while they are attracting one type, they also need to protect themselves against others – ones that eat their leaves, flowers or fruit without helping with pollination.

There's a constant war going on in the forest, between the plants, the insects, the birds and the mammals – one that's difficult for us to unravel.

The castanha-da-galinha tree

THE COMPLEX plant/animal web has been worked out for one Amazonian tree called castanha-de-galinha. Its life-cycle relies on three completely different types of animal, bats, agoutis and ants, and in turn the animals rely on the tree.

In the tropics there are hundreds of species of fruit-bat. They feed on nectar and many different sorts of fruit, and trees that use bats for pollination are specially adapted to help them feed. Unlike our bats, they feed all year round, but visiting different trees at different times, planning their harvest. If one type of tree is felled, the circle is broken, and the bats may die out, even though they are surrounded by trees that supply their food at other times of year, or even by fruit that they cannot reach.

How the circle works
The cycle can be broken at any stage: if the bats' roost is destroyed, the castanha is not pollinated. If the agoutis are frightened away, the seeds are not planted. If the ants' nest is destroyed, the sapling may be eaten by caterpillars or other ants. And if the castanha is felled, the animals lose their food source.

Ants for protection
The most dangerous time for any tree is when it's just starting to grow, making a very tasty snack for any plant-eater. As the castanha saplings grow they secrete nectar from their leaves, to attract ants, which drink the nectar and protect the tree from other insects likely to eat the leaves.

Bats carry pollen
The castanha-de-galinha has flowers that open at night and hang down from the branches in bunches, so that fruit bats can fly up and drink their nectar. In doing so they get covered in pollen, and fly off to the next tree with a vital cargo.

The fruit grows
If the next tree is another castanha, then the flowers will be fertilised. They produce a fleshy egg-shaped fruit, containing the seeds of the next generation.

Planting the seeds
When it's ripe, the fruit falls, and is collected by small mammals called agoutis. Like squirrels, agoutis will hoard food to eat later, burying it in the leaf-litter, but often forget just where they left it. So a new tree may grow from a seed carefully planted by an animal!

WILDSIDE WATCH

- **Every living system has webs and cycles like this, but in the rainforest they are very specific. We have to understand the webs before we can safely exploit them.**
- **In South-East Asia there is a $100 million trade in durian fruit. It's pollinated by bats living in limestone caves. These are being destroyed for cement, ruining a profitable natural harvest.**

Reaching for the sky

AN AVERAGE RAINFOREST tree stands 30 m (100 ft) high and weighs 40 tonnes, yet it stands in soil little richer than sand, and has grown very, very slowly!

It may take 40–50 years for a mahogany tree to reach the canopy, and it never stops growing. A mature tree sheds over 10,000 seeds, providing a food source for insects and rodents. The leaves will be harvested by tree-dwellers, from caterpillars to howler monkeys, and the trunk may provide a home for macaws or marmosets, and be the whole world to a colony of ants.

The life-story

WHEN A SEED hits the ground, its chances of replacing its parent are about 10,000 to one, since only when an old tree collapses will there be a space in the canopy to aim for.

The seeds are much more likely to be eaten by an animal, perhaps a rodent like an acouchi, or a peccary, a striped forest pig. If a seed is left alone and germinates, the ground has to be soft enough for the first root to penetrate, so that it can gather the nutrients for the first leaves. The seed has a supply of food, but this only lasts until the chlorophyll of the first leaves starts to work.

The seedling could be eaten in a few hours by ants, or crushed by a larger animal, but once the leaves start harnessing the sunlight, it has a chance. By the end of its first year, it will be about 10 cm (4 in) tall. After 15 years, it will be a good-sized sapling, and will start to produce flowers.

As it grows, the bottom of the trunk forms buttresses, triangular growths that give the tree stability in the shallow soil. By the age of about 150 it will reach maturity.

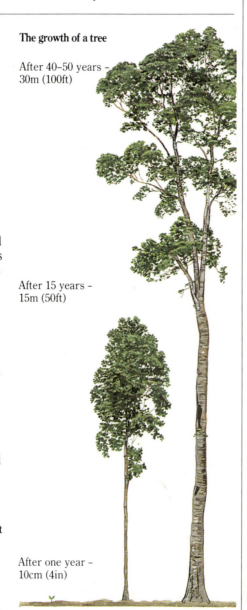

The growth of a tree

After 40–50 years – 30m (100ft)

After 15 years – 15m (50ft)

After one year – 10cm (4in)

Right: Like animals, trees have a natural life-span, often hundreds of years long. Felling cuts it short. Other wildlife depends on the tree, so when it is felled, the whole habitat is destroyed. **Top right:** Mature rainforest trees are huge, and difficult to fit into a photograph! The enormous base of this Madagascan hardwood dwarfs any human being.

Felling the tree

THE FIRST JOB is to cut through the buttress with the chainsaw, cutting a deep V towards the trunk, and breaking the tree's internal support. Then the job of slicing into the trunk begins; sometimes wedges are hammered into the core wood to ease the passage of the ripsaw blade.

Not long after the chainsaw roars into life, there's another, louder noise, as 40 tonnes of tree crashes through the canopy – 100 years of growth are destroyed in 100 minutes. The plants are crushed and the animals have fled or died in the impact.

The tree is now timber – it will be stripped, cut into sections, dragged or floated to a sawmill and cut again. It may form a beautiful piece of furniture, or be pulped for paper, or be used to form a mould for a concrete building, and then be thrown away. But it will never be majestic again.

WILDSIDE WATCH

Wood is everywhere around you.
● When do you use wood? What sort of wood is it? Look around your house, your school, places you visit.
● Look for the symbol of the *Good Wood Guide* and ask where the wood is from.
● Avoid items made of tropical wood. Why not have pine instead?
● A 10 per cent tax on tropical wood could raise millions of pounds to protect the forests.

Plants in mid-air

FOR THE SMALLER plants of the forest, the canopy is a big problem, since it cuts out 75 per cent of the light essential for growth. The plants have three different solutions.

Vines grow fast towards the light, so fast that the trunk cannot support the weight of the leaves. This forces them to climb up the trunks of other trees. Some plants, epiphytes, grow on the trees themselves, with roots that never reach the ground. Some parasitic plants, including the giant Amazon rafflesia, have a third way round the problem – they supplement the process of photosynthesis by trapping and digesting insects.

In the forest

ON ANY RAINFOREST TREE, there may be as many as 100 other plants. The branches are often covered in mosses and ferns, and these provide a bed for larger plants, such as orchids or bromeliads. Orchids store water in fleshy roots, and grow huge dense mats of aerial roots that anchor in the bark, drawing moisture from the air and nutrients from the tree. Eighty per cent of tropical orchids grow like this, as 'epiphytes'.

Bromeliads are relatives of the pineapple, with a tight leaf rosette that may hold 4 litres (7 pints) of rainwater – a pond in mid-air.

Vines grow up the tree trunks, spanning the space of the understorey. Fig seeds often germinate in the crotch of a branch, high above the ground, sending out shoots and roots that will eventually take over the host tree, until it merely supports the fig.

The rainforest plants adapt to life high above ground level, their fate bound up with that of the trees.

Orchid flowers have spectacular shapes and bright colours to attract insects. This one is an epiphyte, growing on a tree branch in the Costa Rican rainforest.

These are typical rainforest houseplants, which can be bought in garden centres and supermarkets.

Parlour palm
A dwarf species of palm, the parlour palm has deeply divided fronds arching from the central stem.

Scarlet star

Bromeliads
The scarlet star and pink urn plant are both bromeliads, relatives of the pineapple. They often have very bright flowers growing out of the centre of the leaf rosette.

Symbidium orchid
Plants of the orchid family have flower spikes in beautiful colours, making them as desirable to humans as they are to useful pollinating insects in the forest.

Rubber plant
Many rainforest species, such as rubber plants and umbrella plants, have thick waxy leaves. In the forest these make the rain run off easily and give extra protection against insects.

Plants at home

MANY OF THE PLANTS in our houses come originally from tropical forests. Rubber plants, umbrella plants, parlour palms and many other foliage types are rainforest species, with a distinctive waxy coating on the leaves.

The 'air plants' that never need watering are rainforest epiphytes. Flowering plants are also imported, and the combined world trade in plants and animals tops £2.5 billion per year, as much as the timber trade. The main plant types are orchids, succulents, bromeliads and cycads – some are imported directly, others are cultivated here, with the wild plants used in breeding new strains. This is the case with the fuchsia, a very common house plant which is cultivated using root-stock from the wilds of Bolivia.

It is estimated that ten per cent of the plant species in the world are traded for horticulture: some 30,000 different species, of which 3000 are orchids. Many of these plants are now becoming rare – a slipper orchid that grows only in a National Park in Borneo was sold for the enormous sum of $10,000 in 1987, having been stolen from the wild!

Spiny vines for furniture

THE FORESTS of South-East Asia are home to a climbing palm called rattan, which produces strong fibrous stems used in cane furniture, baskets, matting etc. The international trade in rattan is second only to the timber trade – Indonesia alone exports 86,000 tonnes of rattan each year.

The rattan is collected by local villagers – no easy task given the sharp spines along the vines – which restricts the scale of the operation. But when the world price increases, there is pressure to cut down more and more rattan.

Products made from rattan

Cane chair

Matting

Basket

WILDSIDE WATCH

Plant trade is monitored by CITES – the Convention on International Trade in Endangered Species. This restricts or bans the trading of certain plants and animals amongst countries that have signed the Convention. But several countries are not members, and the trade goes on.
● **Check the plants in your local garden centre. Do the labels say whether they are home-grown or imported? If not, why not?**

Pink urn plant

Bird's nest fern
Ferns are bought for their rich evergreen foliage. These bird's nest fern leaves slowly unroll from the fibrous core of the plant.

Living leather

RAINFOREST is an ideal habitat for reptiles. They are cold-blooded, so their bodies need a warm environment to work efficiently. Forest rivers are home to alligators and caimans, and large constricting snakes such as pythons and anacondas can move easily through flooded forest areas.

All reptiles have tough, scaly skin, which makes a thin but very strong leather, widely used in the fashion trade.

Leather products

SINCE THE 1950s, supplies of crocodile and alligator skins have come mainly from ranches, with over 100,000 'classic' skins traded legally each year. This does not affect wild populations directly, but it has stimulated the leather trade in other skins. The spectacled caiman is not one of the 'classics' but at least 400,000 are known to die each year. The trade is mainly illegal, so the real figure may be three times higher.

The main importers are makers of fashion shoes and handbags in Italy and France. Enforcing the law in France is difficult, because French Guiana, a former colony in South America, is recognised as part of France. This makes the movement of skins very easy, since they start their journey inside the European Community.

Singapore is one of the centres for animal trade, and many shops sell goods like these snakeskin shoes and bags. The trade takes little notice of the rarity or importance of the animals, only what they are worth as handbags!

This common iguana is not in the wild, but a pet. Live animals may be exported for educational reasons, but many will die for each one exported.

Patterned skins

CROCODILES have the thickest skin of all reptiles, and many snakes have brilliant patterns for camouflage or display, so these are the animals most under threat from the leather trade. All the 21 crocodile species have some form of protection, but the trade, both legal and illegal, still continues and seems out of control.

The spectacled caiman is the victim of a huge, mainly illegal trade. It is a small river crocodile from South America, about 3 m (10 ft) long, and with thick, scaly skin like armour on the back and belly.

The dramatic camouflage patterns of large constricting snakes – boas and pythons – and of lizards such as the tegu lizards, mean they are also killed for their skins, which are more delicate and finer-grained. One type is the tupinambis, a squat, metre-long tegu lizard that eats small mammals, insects and eggs and lives throughout the South American forest.

Trade in tegu skins is controlled by CITES (see page 19), but over a million skins are exported annually through Argentina, and these skins may come originally from anywhere in South America. Most will end up as cowboy boots.

Left: In the wild, spectacled caimans have a simple life – eating frogs, fish and mammals, basking on sandbanks and in this case having their tears sipped by butterflies!

Boa constrictors live both in trees and on the ground, with strong patterns that camouflage them amongst the leaves and leaf-litter. These patterns are the reasons for their use in the fashion trade.

WILDSIDE WATCH

In December 1989, Paraguay allowed trade in reptile skins to resume, and encouraged the export of skin products made in Paraguay, including shoes and handbags, to earn foreign currency.

● **We need shoes, but do they have to be made from wild animal skins?**
● **Each caiman skin earns the hunter only about £3.50. The real money is made between Brazil and your local shops.**
● **If you are in a country where souvenirs and trinkets made from reptiles are available, do not support the trade. Do not buy them.**

Keeping warm?

THE TOP MAMMAL predators of the rainforest are members of the cat family – from the smallest margays up to the largest jaguars. These hunters have little to fear in the forest – they are agile and well-armed enough to catch their prey without risking injury, and during the day their spotted coat is perfect camouflage in the dappled light of the forest.

But that coat is their downfall – because humans want to wear it too.

Small cats at risk

JUST LIKE domestic cats, the small jungle cats are mainly nocturnal tree-climbers. They live alone, with overlapping territories, and hunt for small mammals, birds and the occasional fish.

The largest of the group is the ocelot, which is up to 150 cm (5 ft) from head to tail, and weighs around 15 kg (33 lb). The margay has a similar build but is only two-thirds the size, and the smallest is the Geoffroy's cat which may only be 70 cm (28 in) in length. All have a dense fur coat, which traps a barrier of air to keep the cat's temperature stable, and is beautifully patterned with complex spots called rosettes.

Cat skins have been traded for fashion for generations, starting with cheetah, leopard and jaguar, but moving to small species as the animals became rarer, the costs increased, and laws were introduced to protect the animals.

The problem with moving the target of the trade to the smaller species is that the impact is greater – to make a coat from the skin of a small cat like a margay means trapping and killing between 40 and 50 animals.

Illegal trade

TRADE IN SOME small cat furs is legal under licence from CITES, others are fully protected. In 1975, Britain imported 76,000 cat skins, but since then pressure from conservationists has reduced the trade. Even so, 34,000 skins were imported in 1985 – and that means 34,000 wild animals died for the fashion trade in Britain alone.

The biggest problem is that while some species such as jaguar and ocelot are protected, it is practically impossible to tell the skin of a young, protected ocelot from an adult, tradable margay, so the laws are very difficult to enforce. Another problem is that the animals are caught in the wild using traps – and traps certainly cannot tell whether a cat is protected or not.

Above: These are illegal jaguar and ocelot skins, confiscated in Brazil. How many are there? How many coats would they make? Wouldn't they look much better on living wild animals?
Top left: Jaguars are the biggest cats in the forest, with a stocky, muscular body. They are solitary except in the breeding season, and after mating the females care for a litter of two to four cubs on their own.
Far left: The margay is one of the smallest cats, with large eyes and fine bones. Trade is controlled, but difficult to enforce, and up to 50 of these beautiful animals die to make one coat.
Left: Much of the recent trade has been in ocelots, which have only been protected since 1989. Ocelots are nocturnal, and may hunt right through the night. They eat small mammals, birds and reptiles, and hunt on the ground and in the trees.

WILDSIDE WATCH

Fur coats are no longer as fashionable as they were, but are still sold.
- Should we wear fur at all, when wild animals are killed just for our fashion and vanity?
- Fake furs are an alternative, but they keep the chic image of fur coats alive, so the trade continues, and some is illegal.
- What can you do? Some anti-fur campaigns are violent, but the conservation charity LYNX has a better idea: they run regular 'fur amnesties' where people can hand over unwanted furs.

Paradise lost?

ALL RAINFORESTS are rich in bird life, none more so than the Amazon, which contains 20 per cent of all the world's bird species. There are ground-dwellers, seed-eaters, hawks, eagles and vultures, but the most famous rainforest birds are the parrots.

Parrots live in all the rainforest regions, in Africa, South-East Asia, and the Caribbean. But of the 330 parrot species, 103 are under threat, and 77 are in imminent danger of extinction. Many South American species are sold in the USA, and African species in Europe.

Macaws in the wild

THE LARGEST PARROTS – the macaws – only live in the Amazon. There are 16 species, living on fruit and seeds. They use their huge beaks to crack the toughest seedcoat, and are immune to the tannins and other chemicals produced by the plant to stop the seeds being eaten. They live in a perfect setting – most feed on at least 20 different plant species, and scarlet macaws have been recorded eating 38! Besides flying, they climb around the branches, using the beak like a third hand.

But 600,000 parrots are traded each year. Argentina alone exports 175,000 birds to the pet trade, mainly in the USA, and Guyana now has government quotas to reduce the legal trade to just 37,000 parrots a year, but this is still a vast number.

The hyacinth macaw is one of the most valuable – there are just 2500 in the wild, yet 500 were traded in 1989, with a pair fetching up to £9500.

The problem for hyacinth macaws is that as they get rarer, they become more valuable to collectors. Protection is so difficult that even a total international ban cannot prevent the trade.

Parrots in captivity. They are active, intelligent birds which live up to 80 years. The blue and yellow macaw (right) comes from the Amazon, and has a wingspan of about a metre, the same size as its cage. The African grey (below) is renowned as a talker, copying human sounds and possibly able to understand language. The smaller barred parakeet (bottom) in the white cage is from South America, living in forests from Peru to Panama. Even a parrot in a gold cage is a prisoner unable to fly.

Birds in transit

THE BIRDS ARE stolen from nests or trapped by local people, using decoy birds and glue on the nearby branches. The trappers get £5–10 a bird. It is estimated that about 15 per cent of birds don't survive the trapping process, and a further 20 per cent die while awaiting shipment.

The birds are packed tightly and flown as freight, so any delay in the flight can cause more deaths. 200,000 birds are imported into the UK each year – and government figures record 5000 as dead on arrival, whilst 21,000 die during the quarantine period. The official mortality rate is 13 per cent, but it is thought that the real figure may be as high as 80 per cent – 160,000 birds a year.

Trade like this has pushed the Spix's macaw to extinction. Only one bird is known in the wild, in Bahia State in Brazil, but there are at least 16 in captivity. They are in the hands of collectors, and it is doubtful that these birds will ever breed. So as the species dies out, any left become more valuable.

Senegal parrots in transit. They are trapped in the wild, perhaps by using a maimed bird as a decoy, crammed into boxes and flown to Europe and the United States. Of ten birds caught in the wild, only one may ever reach a pet shop.

WILDSIDE WATCH

In 1984 New York State banned the importing and sale of wild-caught birds. Every country could do the same to discourage this type of pet trade.
- Is there a parrot in your local pet shop? Does it seem happy or not? Was it caught in the wild?
- Can you stop the trade? Join the Royal Society for the Protection of Birds or the international group ICBP who both run campaigns against the trade.

The butterfly trade

RAINFORESTS ARE TEEMING with insects; ants that tidy up the forest floor, beetles that burrow through the tree bark, and butterflies that feed on the nectar of flowers high up in the trees.

Every time an area of rainforest is closely examined, new species of insect appear. The forested country of Panama contains over 1500 different species of butterfly (the United States has 763, Britain just 68!), and a study of 1-hectare plots in the Amazon showed over 200 species per hectare. The plots were in similar rainforest, yet each had a completely different range of species making up its total.

Butterflies have very close relationships with individual plants – as food for their caterpillars, or providing nectar. In return, the butterflies carry pollen between the plants, fertilising the flowers.

The art of display

THE FIRST BUTTERFLY collections were assembled by Victorian explorers. The large, brilliant butterflies were mounted on pins, with their wings spread.

Butterflies stay colourful, even when they are dead. In addition to pigments, they have what are known as 'physical colours', brilliant blues, reds and silver, produced by their scales. The scales have fine ridges, so when light falls on them, it is reflected as colours, even if the butterfly is dead.

To see tropical butterflies flying free in a butterfly house is much better than viewing a mounted specimen, provided they are species not threatened in the wild, or have been bred in captivity. In Papua New Guinea, birdwing butterflies are farmed in the rainforest, and transported safely as dormant pupae. This earns more money for the local people than logging would, and does not harm the forest.

Butterflies in the wild

THE WORLD'S LARGEST and brightest butterflies come from the tropics. They are cold-blooded, so while they can only live in summer in Europe and America, they can fly all year in the rainforest, and grow to a large size.

The Queen Alexandra birdwing butterfly comes from the forests of Papua New Guinea, and the female, which has a 25 cm (10 in) wingspan, is the world's largest butterfly. It is restricted to the rainforest on the coastal plains, and always lays its eggs on one type of plant, a vine that provides food and protection for its caterpillars. The females lay up to 240 eggs, and they take four months to develop through the caterpillar and pupa stages to adulthood.

Left: Tropical butterflies are the biggest and brightest in the world. They fly well in warm, still air and there is always plenty of nectar to drink. This swallowtail looks much better in the wild than it ever could in a collector's tray.
Above left: These pinned butterflies are for sale on a market stall in the Cameron Highlands of Malaysia, and include swallowtails and birdwings.
Below left: The male Queen Alexandra birdwing is much more brightly coloured than the female, but smaller. Trade in this species is now controlled by CITES (see page 19) but unfortunately its habitat is now being destroyed for palm-oil plantations.

WILDSIDE WATCH

Many tropical butterfly species are now protected but the international trade is still enormous.
● If you see a mounted display, how old is it? Should we still take animals from the wild just to pin to our walls?
● In Taiwan, millions of butterflies are made into table mats and other trinkets. Would you buy one?
● Many of our butterflies are under threat too. They're totally dependent on specific food-plants, so by growing butterfly plants, such as buddleia, in your garden you can help them survive.

Big rhinos, small insects

THE RAINFOREST of South-East Asia covers a large number of small countries, from the Malay Peninsula to the 13,000 islands that make up Indonesia, including Borneo and Java. It has an enormous range of plants, mammals, insects and birds, including the birds of paradise of Papua New Guinea.

All are under threat from the felling of the huge dipterocarp trees unique to the region. Malaysia, Sarawak and Borneo all have extensive logging operations, some running round the clock, lit by spotlights. The process is incredibly destructive – three times as many trees are damaged as are felled, and are then left open to disease in a ruined landscape.

Butterflies and caterpillars

IN CONTRAST to this, within the undisturbed forest, all the animals and plants depend on each other, from the smallest insects to the largest mammals. Plants near the riverbank, for example, supply nectar for adult butterflies, and the butterflies move pollen from one flower to another, so the plants can breed.

The vast numbers of both means that butterflies may rely on one individual species of plant, and vice-versa. But their caterpillars can be very destructive: as they develop, they can eat their body weight in leaves thousands of times over.

Many plants protect themselves by producing poisons, but some caterpillars carry on eating, storing the poisons in defensive hairs to protect themselves from predators. To advertise this chemical weaponry, they have developed skins of bright red and yellow warning colours!

Right: Living on a diet of pure sugar does have drawbacks. These phoebis butterflies need salts as well, and drink from soil or animal urine.

Rhinos at risk

THE RIVERBANK also attracts an animal at the opposite end of the scale, because the dense forests are home to two species of leaf-eating rhino. The two-horned Sumatran rhino is the smaller. There are less than 1000 of them living in Malaysia and some of the islands.

The larger single-horned Javan rhino is now on the verge of extinction. The only viable population is 50–70 animals living in the Ujung Kulon National Park in Java. When a group is as small as this, disease or a hurricane could easily wipe out the species.

Although the rhinos are in a wild reserve, they are still vulnerable to poachers. Since 1985 at least two animals have been killed for their rare and now very valuable horn. To prevent extinction, there are plans to use the park as a 'megazoo' and increase protection for the rhinos, or to capture some and set up a new colony as an insurance policy.

Above: Chinese folk-medicine claims that powdered rhino horn is a cure for various ills, with Asian horn valued much higher than African types. This maintains the price for illegal horn.
Left: This female Sumatran rhino is enjoying a wallow. The mud will keep her skin supple, and when it dries and drops off, it takes any skin parasites with it. She is the rarest mammal pictured in this book.

WILDSIDE WATCH

The rainforest in South-East Asia has many problems, not just of poaching, which are often edged out of the news by stories from Brazil. Often the problems are greater, especially since they are usually caused by multinational companies rather than government agencies.
● African rhinos are also threatened by poaching, and you can support schemes that help to protect them.
● The Surabaya Zoo on Java is co-operating with some American zoos in captive-breeding Sumatran rhinos. There's a long way to go, but scientific study and captive breeding may help to save the species, which otherwise might well be heading for extinction.

Old men of the forest

'ORANG-UTAN' means 'forest man' – a suitable name for the largest of the tree-dwelling apes, since a large male can weigh 90 kg (200 lb).

Orangs live on the islands of Sumatra and Borneo, climbing around the vines and saplings of the forest understorey. They sway across gaps rather than jumping, and use their hands and feet to grasp for branches as they climb around.

It is thought that there are about 150,000 wild orang-utans, but only about 20,000 are safely protected from logging operations and other deforestation.

A natural zoo

IN KALIMANTAN, Borneo, biologist Birute Galdikas has been studying the local orang-utans since 1971. She has also re-introduced over 50 young orangs orphaned by logging operations or stolen from the wild. The scheme is controversial, since it introduces animals alien to that particular place, but the orangs are more used to humans, and easier to see than in their entirely wild habitat, so the area is also a very natural zoo.

Birute Galdikas with a young orang at her rehabilitation centre.

Living naturally

ADULT MALES are twice the size of the females, and live a solitary existence, keeping their distance from other males by calling, and maintaining a large territory that may include several females. The females give birth to a single baby three or four times a lifetime. The young are carried around by their mother for the first five years, then follow her through the forest until they are about ten, and are mature.

The orang's daily routine starts shortly after dawn. They forage through the forest, mainly harvesting fruit as well as nuts, leaves and bark, and occasionally insects or eggs. At night they build a temporary nest in the trees, taking 20–30 minutes to build a stable platform of branches, sometimes even including a roof to keep the rain out. These apes are very intelligent animals, able to remember details of their territories, and predict the fruiting of particular trees.

Orang-utans in the forest
Orangs live quiet lives several metres off the ground (below). Being vegetarian, they are surrounded by food, and they have no natural enemies. They simply spend the day moving from one meal to the next, passing from tree to tree by reaching across the gaps with their long arms. This means they can only live in dense forest.

Orangs have been kept in captivity since 1776, and their human-like faces and expressions make them very popular. Many are kept in concrete enclosures – easy to clean, but not much like a rainforest.

In captivity

DURING THE 1960s and 1970s, the trade in orang-utans for zoos and as pets was a major problem. The mothers were killed and the youngsters taken, but as with most animal trade, several orangs died for every one successfully traded. There is still illegal international trade – nine young orangs were confiscated by customs officers in Taiwan in September 1990.

Since 1928 nearly 900 orangs have been born in captivity, and although many have died young, others have survived to over 40 years old.

The main problem is housing. Orangs live in the wild in harmony with a complex environment, harvesting the fruit and travelling through a territory that may cover several square kilometres, although they only move a few hundred metres each day. Too often the zoo conditions are designed for convenience and bear no relation to their natural environment.

WILDSIDE WATCH

The WWF runs a fund-raising scheme called the Global Primate Campaign, which includes a programme for orangs in Indonesia.
● Is there an orang-utan in your local zoo? What is the enclosure like?
● Conservationists in Indonesia and Malaysia have won protection for the orangs, with reserves established in Sumatra, Borneo and Sarawak. But land-clearing reaches to the edge of the reserves . . .

A future in the trees?

ONE OF THE MOST distinctive sounds of dawn in an Asian rainforest is the calling of the gibbons – a loud, whooping, siren-like call. They are the smallest species of ape, and they live high in the canopy, swinging from branch to branch on their very long arms.

Gibbons never come down to the ground, and need a good hand-hold every few metres, so they can only live in dense forest. Any breaks in the forest cover, made by roads or logging camps, can ruin a whole area for them.

Grey gibbons
Grey gibbons are particularly at risk. They live in Sarawak, where logging is a huge industry, carving up the rainforest day and night, and leaving them nowhere to live.

Nowhere to go

NINETY PER CENT of all primate species live in rainforests around the world. Tarsiers, lemurs, monkeys and apes are all hit by the destruction of their habitat, particularly in parts of South-East Asia.

The tree canopy is their home and it needs to remain undisturbed for them to flourish. The grey gibbon is under the greatest threat from intensive logging in the Malaysian state of Sarawak, on the island of Borneo. At present, Malaysia exports two-thirds of the world's hardwood logs, and Sarawak alone exports 15 times more wood than any other country.

Carving up the rainforest

LOGGING OPERATIONS in South-East Asia are 'selective' – only taking the large dipterocarp trees. But in a logging area, 14 per cent of the forest is destroyed for roads, and 27 per cent for dragging the logs to the roads – so it ruins the whole area for animals.

Gibbons live in pairs, with a single baby born every three to four years. They swing through the forest to forage for leaves and fruit such as figs. They'll eat any insects that they find.

Each family has its own territory of up to half a square kilometre, surrounded by other families. Roads and tracks carve up these areas and wholly or partly destroy their territory, trapping the gibbons on one side of the road. They either die out or have to move, struggling for new territory with neighbouring gibbons, something that would never happen naturally.

Lar gibbons
Lar gibbons are one of the most widespread species, living in mainland Malaysia, Thailand and northern Sumatra. Since 1975 their numbers have been dramatically reduced as their habitat has been destroyed.

Road systems
With the biggest trees deep in the forest, roads are needed to transport the logs to sawmills or towns. Peasant villages spring up beside the road, and it cannot be crossed by any animal that lives only in the trees, so the forest is changed completely.

WILDSIDE WATCH

The gibbon story shows that measuring destruction by area can be misleading – even a narrow road can be catastrophic.
● Did you know that logging earns Sarawak £2.5 million a year? When local people protested about the destruction, many were jailed – so who benefits?
● Profitable trees are spread out through the forest, but 'selective forestry' is a myth, because bulldozers aren't selective. Once the loggers arrive, the wildlife always suffers.

Forests under the sea

WHERE THE FOREST meets the sea, there is an extraordinary habitat of trees that live in black mud starved of oxygen, and with their roots covered in salt water – enough to kill off most other plants!

This is a mangrove swamp. It is found all over the tropics, and like inland rainforest, it is rich in wildlife. As in the main forest, the basis for all the wildlife is the trees, which form zones depending on how well they tolerate salt water. The trees live in a delicate balance with the sea, and any change in the system can be catastrophic.

In the mangroves

THE ZONE nearest the sea has pioneer species of tough shrubs with roots at water level that catch the silt and sand washing around with the tide. Since there is no oxygen in the mud, the roots poke out of the mud into the air, where they are able to absorb the oxygen directly.

The next zone has trees with 'stilt-roots' growing out of the trunk. These spread outwards to support the tree against the tide, and trap more silt.

The mangroves are home to some extraordinary animals, including the proboscis monkey of Borneo, mudskipper fish that walk about on land and crab-eating frogs. The roots act as breakwaters, reducing the power of the waves, so the water around them is rich in young fish, crabs and prawns. These in turn provide an abundant food supply which attracts a rich bird-life.

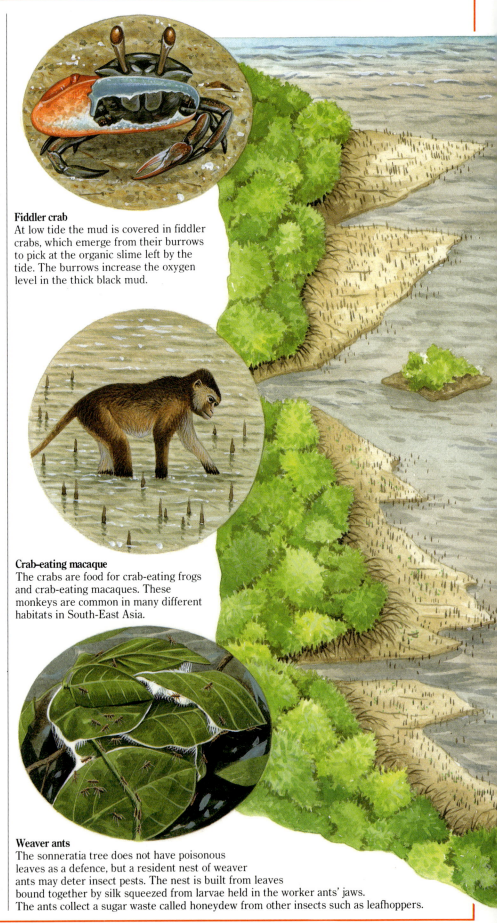

Fiddler crab
At low tide the mud is covered in fiddler crabs, which emerge from their burrows to pick at the organic slime left by the tide. The burrows increase the oxygen level in the thick black mud.

Crab-eating macaque
The crabs are food for crab-eating frogs and crab-eating macaques. These monkeys are common in many different habitats in South-East Asia.

Weaver ants
The sonneratia tree does not have poisonous leaves as a defence, but a resident nest of weaver ants may deter insect pests. The nest is built from leaves bound together by silk squeezed from larvae held in the worker ants' jaws. The ants collect a sugar waste called honeydew from other insects such as leafhoppers.

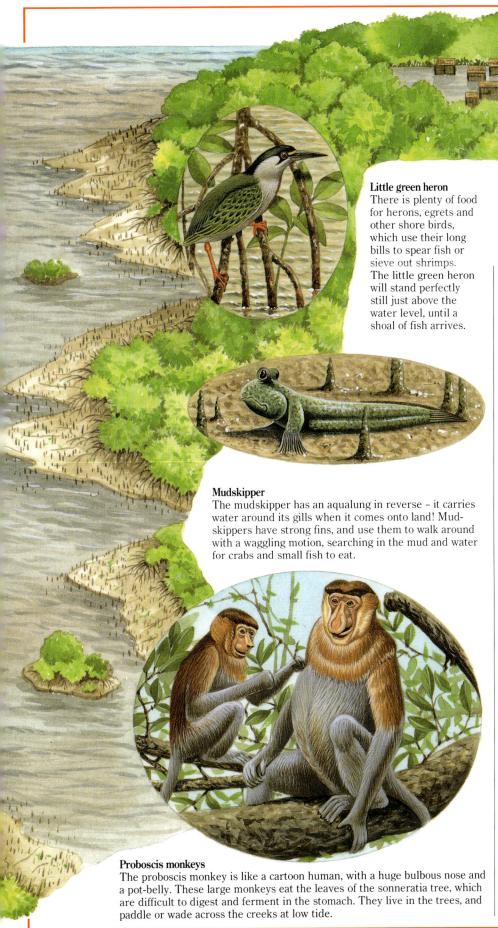

Little green heron
There is plenty of food for herons, egrets and other shore birds, which use their long bills to spear fish or sieve out shrimps. The little green heron will stand perfectly still just above the water level, until a shoal of fish arrives.

Mudskipper
The mudskipper has an aqualung in reverse – it carries water around its gills when it comes onto land! Mudskippers have strong fins, and use them to walk around with a waggling motion, searching in the mud and water for crabs and small fish to eat.

Proboscis monkeys
The proboscis monkey is like a cartoon human, with a huge bulbous nose and a pot-belly. These large monkeys eat the leaves of the sonneratia tree, which are difficult to digest and ferment in the stomach. They live in the trees, and paddle or wade across the creeks at low tide.

Fish farming
The water around the mangroves is teeming with the larvae of crabs, fish and prawns. In Ecuador and the Philippines, fish farms are a common cause of mangrove destruction, with artificial ponds replacing the natural creeks.

Threats

MANGROVE SWAMPS are often seen as wastelands, ripe for any form of exploitation, and they are now being destroyed at an alarming rate, without the publicity that has accompanied similar destruction in the main rainforests.

The problems are different in different parts of the world. In Africa, it is mainly clear-felling by slash-and-burn farmers, who use the wood for fuel, and plant rice paddies on the shore.

In over-populated areas reclamation for housing is the problem. In Singapore the forest has been reduced to about 7 per cent of its original area.

In the Philippines it's fish-farming. Areas are cleared to make ponds for fish and prawns – a profitable use of the 'waste land'. At the current rate of loss, all the Philippine mangroves will disappear before the year 2000.

WILDSIDE WATCH

The mangroves suffer a typical problem. We think of them as wasteland, but they are a well balanced ecological system.
● There is probably 'waste' land around you. What actually lives there?
● If we measure everything by profit, many natural areas are worthless. But the floods in Bangladesh kill thousands of people and disaster relief costs millions of pounds. Spending the money to protect the mangroves that are a natural defence could be cheaper!

The endangered

MADAGASCAR is an island in two senses – it lies off the eastern coast of Africa, and its wildlife has been isolated for over 100 million years. This gives the rainforests on its eastern seaboard a unique wildlife, dominated by 29 species of lemur, primitive primates replaced elsewhere by monkeys.

Almost 50 per cent of the rainforest, which once covered half the island, has already been cleared, but the relatively small size of Madagascar means that monitoring and protection of the habitat is possible: it's a problem small enough for us to grasp and may provide the template for future forest-protection schemes.

The wildlife

MADAGASCAR is only twice the area of Britain, but has 8500 known plant species, 80 per cent of which are found nowhere else on earth. The vast majority too of its frogs, reptiles and mammals are found nowhere else – and there are more chameleon species in Madagascar than the rest of the world put together.

The forests are home for lemurs, primitive primates that have survived because the island separated from Africa before monkeys evolved. The smallest, the mouse-lemur, is just 15 cm (6 in) long, and the largest, the indri, is larger than many monkeys. Ring-tailed lemurs live in groups on the ground, but others spend most of their time in the trees.

The rarest of all lemurs is the aye-aye, a nocturnal lemur that hunts for insects' larvae by listening for their movements under tree-bark, and has a long thin third finger for probing them out. The 'newest' lemur is the golden bamboo lemur, which was only discovered in 1986. All these species are threatened by deforestation.

island

Main picture: Sifakas are large lemurs that live high in the trees. They have very long legs for leaping between branches, covering several metres in one bound.
Above left: Indris are the largest lemurs, famous for their loud calls. These are used for defending their territory, which may be very extensive, and for keeping contact amongst the group.
Above: Ring-tailed lemurs feed in the trees, but often travel around on the ground. The black-and-white striped tail is both a visual signal and covered in the animal's scent.

The plan

MADAGASCAR is a poor country, partly due to the low price of its main export, coffee. Most people live in rural areas, where forest clearances have caused flooding and loss of topsoil.

The plan from the World Bank is to invest $15 million per year for thirty years in reforestation, soil conservation, improved environmental protection and better farming methods.

The rainforest could be harvested: there are 50 species related to commercial coffee, including some that are naturally caffeine-free and could become future natural crops. The plan also allows $3 million per year solely for protecting the wildlife, under the guidance of the Worldwide Fund for Nature (WWF). The pressures on Madagascar are immense, but so is the will to save this unique forest.

Cleared forest areas often suffer from erosion. The trees soften the effect of rain, and when they are gone rainfall sweeps away the good topsoil, leaving deep gulleys and land useless for crops.

WILDSIDE WATCH

● Can you find out more about Madagascar? The farmers earn very little and so use whatever they can find for free, even if they know it's destructive. Economic packages like the Madagascar one are as vital as wildlife rangers for protecting animals.
● Help save this unique rainforest! The wildlife side is under the control of WWF so join the organisation and support their campaign.

Jungle action

AUSTRALIA is unique – a developed country with areas of tropical rainforest. When so much rainforest destruction is caused by poor people desperate to make money or improve their standard of living, surely there should be no destruction of the forests of wealthy Australia? In fact there is, and the public outcry against it is the strongest anywhere in the world. Environmental activists swim in the path of ships carrying logs, stand in front of trucks heading for sawmills, and even sit in trees that are being felled.

Problems and protests

THE GREATER DAINTREE forest is the most important area, and was the scene of the first big campaign. In 1984 it was threatened with felling for timber, sugar-cane farms, small-scale tin-mining, housing, and by a road project. Protesters buried themselves in the path of bulldozers, chained themselves to trees and eventually succeeded in protecting the area.

The rainforest in Northern Queensland has been listed as a World Heritage site. But it is now threatened by a hydro-electric dam on the Tully river south of Cairns, which would flood over 4000 hectares (10,000 acres) of forest. Queensland's output of electricity is already greater than the demand, and energy conservation could save more than the output of the new dam at one-tenth of the cost!

Right: Australia's forests are different from others in South-East Asia – they are a very special habitat well worth protecting. This is one of the Daintree protests, many of which involved both white and aboriginal Australians.

Australia's forest

THE NORTHERN AREAS of Australia's forests are true tropical rainforest, with a dense canopy 30 m (100 ft) up, and vines and epiphytes filling the understorey. They contain 1100 different tree species, and up to 50 different species of epiphyte on one tree. They are home to some of the oldest flowering plants.

There are fruit-eating tree kangaroos, possums and sugar-gliders. There is a huge range of birds, including lorikeets (a type of parrot), sunbirds and large flightless birds called cassowaries. The butterfly population in the forest makes up 62 per cent of Australia's species, including the world's largest butterfly – the Queen Alexandra birdwing.

When Europeans first settled in Australia, about one per cent of the land was rainforest. Since then, 75 per cent of that area has been cleared, and what's left is often very patchy.

Far left: Most kangaroos are adapted for life hopping across flat, even ground, but the Bennett's tree kangaroo lives in trees. It has strong arms and broad feet to help it climb, and lives on fruit and flowers.
Middle left: The sugar glider is a nocturnal possum, with a flap of skin between its front and back legs for gliding. It lives on sugary nectar and fruit.
Left: The cassowary is a large, flightless bird, like an emu but with bright red and blue skin on its neck. The horny crest may be used for parting the vegetation when it runs through the undergrowth.

WILDSIDE WATCH

Developed countries can afford to protect their natural areas, but often there is a conflict of interests. In Australia, the individual state government may want exploitation, while the country's central government wants protection.
● Protest can work – if there's something you want to protect, you can argue your case with the people who make decisions: politicians and businessmen.
● Should there be areas left entirely to the animals where we never enter? That is what a wilderness really is. But it means that you would never see the animals that live there.

A watery wilderness

PART OF the definition of rainforest is that over 300 cm (120 in) of rain falls each year. So water is a vital part of the forest, and all the largest areas are based on very extensive river systems – the Amazon, Zaire and Mekong.

The variety of animals in the trees is mirrored in the water, and the water life is just as sensitive to change as the wildlife on land. Water pollution, or an increase in the level of silt in the water, can alter the balance and wipe out populations of plants and animals which depend on the water and on each other.

Floods and poisons

FOR SIX MONTHS of the year, the areas along the larger tributaries of the Amazon are flooded, as the melted ice of the Andes mountains is carried towards the Atlantic. The flood waters may reach 10 m (33 ft), with only the tops of the trees staying clear. Some flooded trees die, but the flood is a regular, natural event, so the forest keeps growing. Many plants even cast their seeds into the water, to be carried to new areas.

There are over 2000 species of fish, which are the food for many animals, particularly turtles, snakes and birds. The river system is a vital part of the life of the whole forest, and pollution from sawmills, factories or mining can easily upset the balance.

The rivers of the northern Amazon are 'blackwater' rivers, acidic, and stained by the tannins from leaves, but they still support a lot of wildlife. This is the scene for a peasant gold-rush, which involves washing and extraction with highly toxic mercury. With no pollution controls, and mercury levels already six times the safe limit, poisoning is set to become a major problem.

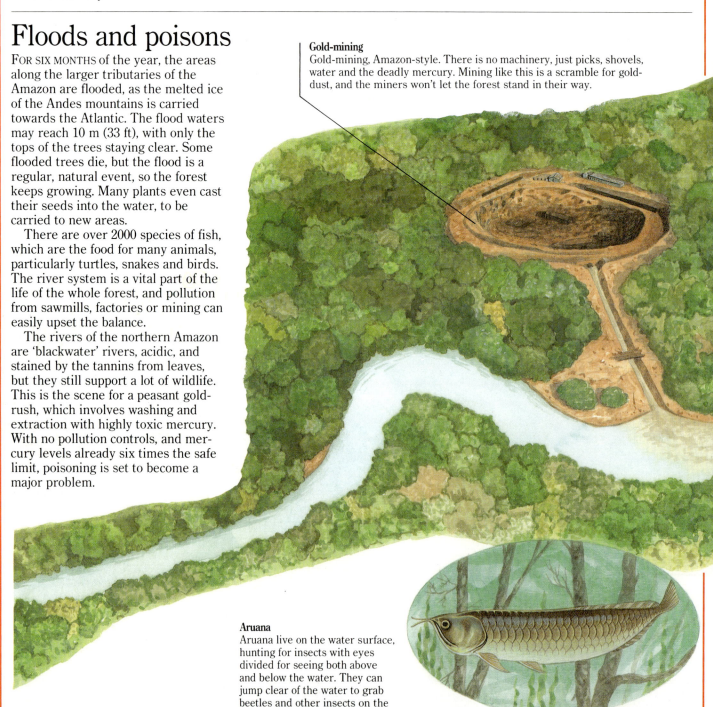

Gold-mining
Gold-mining, Amazon-style. There is no machinery, just picks, shovels, water and the deadly mercury. Mining like this is a scramble for gold-dust, and the miners won't let the forest stand in their way.

Aruana
Aruana live on the water surface, hunting for insects with eyes divided for seeing both above and below the water. They can jump clear of the water to grab beetles and other insects on the plants at the water's edge.

Knife-fish
The knife-fish moves by waving its fins, but keeping its body straight, because it acts as an aerial. It sends out electrical pulses through the water, and detects changes to these electrical fields caused by other animals – a type of underwater radar. They live in silty rivers, and hunt at night, so this method is ideal.

Side-necked turtle
Amazonian turtles belong to a strange group called side-necked turtles, because instead of retracting their neck backwards into the shell, they can only move it to one side. This makes them very vulnerable on land, so they are mainly aquatic.

Logging factory
There are few pollution controls in the Amazon, so any factory or sawmill will discharge oils and chemicals into the water, using the river as a sewer.

Piranha
Piranha have a reputation as meat-eaters. They have very sharp teeth and some species swim in large, dangerous shoals, but most live by nipping scales and fins from large fish, and are only minor predators.

Kingfisher
Kingfishers are common along the smaller rivers, nesting in sandbanks and fishing from perches just above the surface. Unlike other fishing birds, they can be found in the poor waters of 'blackwater' rivers in the north of the Amazon basin. Kingfishers are more common in Europe and Asia, and there are just five species in South America, all of which fish in the Amazon.

WILDSIDE WATCH

Gold-mining in Amazonia has unleashed all sorts of problems.
- The gold-rush has attracted 40,000 miners to the region.
- The reservation of the Yanomami Indians has been invaded and they are in danger from disease and exploitation.
- Using mercury has been banned, but the law is unenforceable. Mercury poisoning could kill two million people over the next ten years.

Damming the rivers

As THE RIVER develops, there's enough space for large predatory fish, turtles, anacondas, birds and dolphins to swim in the open water or fish from the banks. Millions of litres of water flow gently seaward, attracting Brazilian electricity companies setting up hydro-electric schemes.

These schemes need a constant water supply through dams. Every dam has a huge flooded area behind it, and the natural balance of the forest is ruined.

Disaster!

THE DESTRUCTION involved in dam-building is immense, but the problem is made worse when the dam itself is ineffective.

The Balbina Dam north of Manaus in Brazil is a classic. It flooded a vast area, wiping out most of the wildlife, since a rescue operation was very difficult. The lake it formed is only a few metres deep, and is full of stagnant water clogged with rotting vegetation, because the trees, worth £200 million, were not felled before flooding. It is not even economic – its electricity costs the same as that produced by solar power, a much greener option.

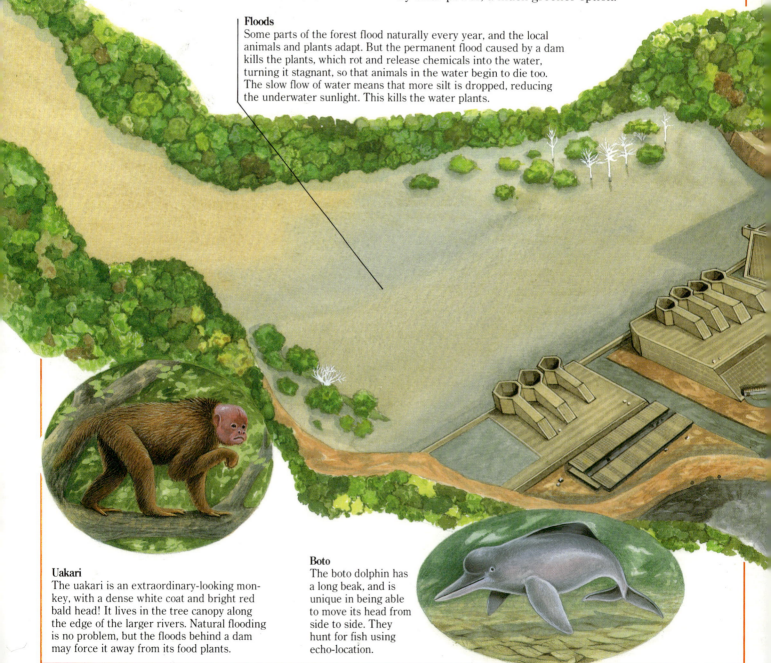

Floods
Some parts of the forest flood naturally every year, and the local animals and plants adapt. But the permanent flood caused by a dam kills the plants, which rot and release chemicals into the water, turning it stagnant, so that animals in the water begin to die too. The slow flow of water means that more silt is dropped, reducing the underwater sunlight. This kills the water plants.

Uakari
The uakari is an extraordinary-looking monkey, with a dense white coat and bright red bald head! It lives in the tree canopy along the edge of the larger rivers. Natural flooding is no problem, but the floods behind a dam may force it away from its food plants.

Boto
The boto dolphin has a long beak, and is unique in being able to move its head from side to side. They hunt for fish using echo-location.

Dam
In Europe, dams are usually built around waterfalls, where the energy of the falling water drives the turbines. In the Amazon, the water has to be forced through the dam, and much more water is needed. So both the dams and the areas of destroyed rainforest are huge.

Skimmer
Skimmers nest on the sandbanks of larger rivers, often in mixed groups with terns. Their lower jaw is longer than the upper, and they fish by flying with the beak open like scissors, and the lower jaw just under the surface. When the beak touches a fish, it snaps shut! Flooding will destroy their nesting grounds.

Tartaruga
The largest Amazon turtle is the tartaruga. Like the marine turtles, they nest communally, coming out of the water onto sand bars and scraping a hole for their 100 or so eggs. The young hatch together, and scramble madly past predators to the safety of the water.

Anaconda
Most of the 160 species of Amazonian snake are aquatic, and the largest is the anaconda. They have a thick body that can grow to over 10m (33ft) long, making them the biggest snakes in the world. Such a bulky body is much easier to move in water.

WILDSIDE WATCH

Modern society uses huge amounts of electricity. We must find ways of using less, and of generating power with less ecological damage.
● Find out more about floods. Tree-felling in the highlands erodes the soil, which causes silting up of the rivers and flooding, as in Bangladesh and Thailand in recent years.
● Support campaigns against uneconomic and particularly destructive dams. But remember that some are carefully planned and efficient.

Giants in danger

THE RIVER SYSTEMS are vital for the larger mammals of the jungle, because getting through thick vegetation is difficult, and rivers provide the only way of easily moving around. Changes to the rivers, whether through damming or pollution from mining and factories, are bound to affect these animals too.

In the Amazon forest there are not very many different types of large mammal – jaguars are the largest cats, and tapirs the largest hoofed mammals. So some of the smaller mammal types have increased in size here, including the world's biggest rodent, the capybara, and the giant otter.

Otters at large

OTTERS ARE SLENDER, swimming carnivores, related to stoats and weasels, but unique in living on fish and other aquatic animals. The familiar short-clawed otters are quite small, but the Amazon giant otters really live up to their name, being almost 2 m (6 ft 6 in) from head to tail. The pregnant females will nest in a hole on the riverbank, but otherwise they live out in the open, fishing and grooming their fur – unfortunately easy prey for trappers.

Once they were quite common throughout the Amazon basin, from the Andes north to Colombia and south to Argentina, but now their population is reduced to small pockets within this range. They have been hunted in the past for their thick fur: more than 20,000 animals were killed for their skins in the 1960s in Brazil alone. There is now both local protection and a CITES ban on trade, yet some poaching still occurs.

Above: Giant otters fish during the day and lie up in specially cleared areas on the river bank, where they scent-mark their landing stage to show ownership.
Right: The tapir's stocky body and wedge-shaped head are ideal for pushing through the rainforest. Its large feet spread its body weight for walking on marshy ground. It is a good swimmer.
Below: The capybara is the world's biggest rodent, larger than many deer. It lives on water plants and swims with slightly webbed feet, keeping its eyes and ears above the surface.

Long noses

TAPIRS are amongst the strangest and most primitive large mammals, unchanged for the last 20 million years. They live in the forests of Malaysia and South America, eating grass, twigs and leaves, pulling food into the mouth using a short proboscis like a miniature elephants' trunk. They feed at night on the open riverbanks, and spend a lot of the daytime in the water – keeping cool, protected from parasites and predators, and casually browsing on water-plants.

Now man is taking over the forest and the tapirs are in danger. They are shot as cheap meat, their skins are used for leather, and their home ranges are flooded by dams. No one knows how many there are, but they are certainly threatened by forest destruction.

WILDSIDE WATCH

● Giant otters are under a greater threat from poachers than the spotted cats, since they live in the open and are easy to find and trap, yet there is very little publicity at present about their plight.
● Otters are under threat in Britain as well. They are easily disturbed, and affected by water pollution.
● The Otter Trust at Bungay in Suffolk is involved in protecting otters, and can give you information about how you can help.

Lying low

EVERY DAY, thousands of animals die in the rainforests, perfectly naturally. The ecosystem is a mass of relationships – between plants and animals, predators and prey. Insects are by far the most numerous animals, eating the plants, or often each other.

Some species, such as butterflies, rely on specific plants for food. Some ants protect the plants they live on in return for a good nest site. Insects are also food for all sorts of other animals from frogs to orang-utans. Avoiding being something else's breakfast is very important for them, so they have evolved some brilliant means of camouflage.

Bugs and beetles

THERE ARE more species of insect in the forests than any other type of animal – so many that we don't know the exact number. Each survey uncovers species new to science, with single trees providing a home for hundreds of different species.

They range from tiny bugs that live inside leaves through hordes of ants and termites to the huge beetles and stick insects up to 33 cm (13 in) long.

Most insects eat plants, and are a vital part of the forest food chain that connects the simplest plants to the biggest carnivores such as jaguars and anacondas.

Right: Spot the insect! The spiny legs of this forest katydid, a type of grasshopper, help it to hide amongst the epiphytic moss on a palm-tree.

How forest camouflage works

AN INSECT SKELETON is a series of tubes, joined together with flexible joints, on the *outside* of the animal. This means that forming the body into an extraordinary shape for camouflage is quite easy, since none of the vital organs inside are affected. There are grasshoppers and moths that look like leaves, mantids that look like flowers, and even a moth caterpillar that looks like a snake.

Frogs don't have the same ability to adapt their body shape, but their thin skin contains sacs of green, brown and even red pigment. This gives them control over their colour to match perfectly with the leaves around them.

The most effective camouflage for a snake is to use its long thin shape to mimic a woody branch or a green twig. The bigger tree-snakes such as tree-boas have mottled camouflage patterns, while the pencil-thin vine snakes are pure green.

Above: This butterfly from the eastern coast of Brazil is the perfect shape and colour to mimic a dead leaf, complete with a missing piece.
Left: A leaf litter toad looks exactly like the dead leaves surrounding it in the forest of Costa Rica.
Below left: The patterned skin of this python coiled up at an Indonesian waterhole makes it very difficult to spot.

WILDSIDE WATCH

Before you can protect any environment, you have to know how the animals interact.
● In order to protect large animals, it's vital to protect their food supply, so even tiny animals are important.
● There are millions of insect species – one in four animals is a beetle!
● Ninety per cent of the insects collected in any rainforest sample may be new to science. We just don't know how many different species there are.

Into the darkness

ALTHOUGH many animals protect themselves by hiding in the forest, others stay alive by only being active at night. In fact it is thought that 80 per cent of animal activity takes place at night. This means that a human perception of the forest, which is normally gained during the daytime, can be completely wrong.

One group of animals that are always nocturnal are the simple primates such as tarsiers and bush-babies. For them a nocturnal life is best for avoiding predators and for feeding on insects, which are slower-moving and easier to catch in the cool of the night.

Red colobus monkeys
Red colobus monkeys are active during the day, feeding on leaves and fruit high in the trees. Some groups are threatened with extinction.

Day and night

AROUND the Equator the day is always equally divided between twelve hours of day and twelve of night, with a very short period of twilight.

In a rainforest like this, in Zaire, the trees are cleared during the day. The biggest pressure is from peasant farmers, who slash and burn the undergrowth and fell the trees in order to plant crops, either as food for themselves or as cash crops to sell.

At night the humans disappear and the animals come out. In the African forest they are bushbabies and pottos, but other rainforests have similar species: the tarsiers in Asia or phalangers in Australia.

Humans
The problem for Africa's rainforest is from peasant farmers, desperate for land to feed their families. They only burn small areas each to plant food crops, but there are so many of them that the total effect is enormous. Less than 4 per cent of African forests are protected.

Fruit bat
The African night is shared with fruit bats, which feed on the fruit of figs and guava. The largest species pick the fruit and carry it off to eat.

Eating gum
Many forest trees have sap in the form of gum, a tacky, sugary substance. The bushbabies strip the bark with their teeth, then lap up the gum underneath.

Leaping bushbaby
Bushbabies move around by making great leaps from tree to tree – in total darkness! They have long legs, and a long tail for balancing, and their senses are adapted for night. They have very large eyes, with a reflecting layer called a 'tapetum' to trap as much light as possible. Their hearing and smell are both keen, to allow them to track insects and sniff out ripe fruit.

Potto
Pottos are related to bushbabies, but climb around rather than leap. They don't need the long hind legs and long tail, so all their limbs are the same length, with an opposable thumb that forms a gripping hand just like ours. They move very slowly, and will stay completely still if threatened, hidden by the folliage around them. Their vision is not as good as the bushbabies', and they feed mainly on insects.

Swaying for insects
The larger species such as the thick-tailed bushbaby eat mainly fruit and gum, but the smaller ones eat more insects. They can catch moths and grasshoppers as they fly past, by anchoring their hind legs to a tree and swaying out into space with their body and arms!

WILDSIDE WATCH

African rainforests are fast disappearing as the human population increases, especially in the Ivory Coast and Nigeria.
- The Guinean rainforest nations of Africa have the highest population growth rate in the world: in 1987 there were 146 million people, by 2020 there will be 370 million.
- Farmers cause 70 per cent of African forest destruction.
- Africa could feed itself, but towns and businesses push the farmers off the good land into the margins of the forest.

An eagle's domain

BUSH-BABIES, flying squirrels and tarsiers are in their turn prey to eagles. The rainforest is home for the world's largest eagles, the harpy eagle and the Philippine eagle. These are the top predators in the forest, and indicators for the whole environment – if the eagles do well, there must be plenty of other wildlife.

The Philippine eagle is one of the 12 most critically endangered species. There are just 300 left in the wild, drastically reduced in numbers by the rapid clearance of their habitat.

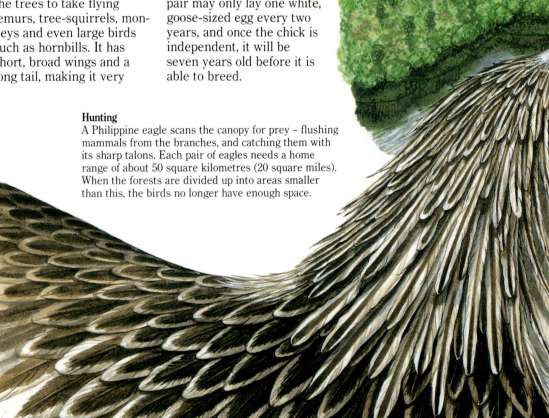

Monkeys
Long-tailed macaque monkeys live in groups high in the trees, feeding on fruit and insects. Those feeding in the tree-tops are targets for the eagles.

How they live

AN ADULT EAGLE has a wingspan of 2.2m (7 ft 6 in), and may weigh 7 kg (15 lb). It can soar above the canopy, but hunts by plunging into the trees to take flying lemurs, tree-squirrels, monkeys and even large birds such as hornbills. It has short, broad wings and a long tail, making it very manoeuvrable amongst the canopy branches.

Like many endangered animals, the eagles breed very slowly, and cannot cope with sudden changes brought by man. A breeding pair may only lay one white, goose-sized egg every two years, and once the chick is independent, it will be seven years old before it is able to breed.

Hunting
A Philippine eagle scans the canopy for prey – flushing mammals from the branches, and catching them with its sharp talons. Each pair of eagles needs a home range of about 50 square kilometres (20 square miles). When the forests are divided up into areas smaller than this, the birds no longer have enough space.

Nest
The eagles nest on platforms of epiphytes in the topmost branches, building a huge stick nest and lining it with greenery when incubating eggs.

Butterflies
The eagle can be a figurehead for wider conservation. The ranges of three species of endangered swallowtail butterflies overlap with that of the eagles, so creating an eagle reserve should help the butterflies too!

Eagles at risk

A BIRD LIKE THIS relies on a healthy environment. The clearance of the forest has left just three islands of the 2000 in the Philippines with enough mammals to support the eagles: these are the islands of Mindanao, Luzon and Palawan.

Other threatened species, including large swallowtail butterflies, need the same sort of forest, and so will benefit too if the eagles can be protected. This makes them a sort of figurehead for the protection of all forest species. The Mount Apo National Park is one of their last strongholds, and the site of a captive-breeding scheme (that has yet to produce a chick).

Man in the forest
Man has had an enormous effect on the forest in the last 50 years. In the Philippines 75 per cent of the forest has been felled, partly for agriculture but mainly for the timber trade.

WILDSIDE WATCH

We can't protect an animal by building a wall around it; we have to protect its food supply, right down to the insects.
● There are currently 17 Philippine eagles in captivity, but there is very little possibility of breeding them.
● A new scheme to save the eagle involves sponsoring the local people to protect them, paying £200 for every nestling that leaves the nest in the area. One such nest is sponsored by the UK Hawk Trust.

Fleeing the fires

IN THE RAINFOREST fires are a rare but natural event, caused by lightning strikes. They have a natural course, and eventually die out, perhaps when the flames hit a river they cannot blow across. For the animals, fire will either be a minor problem or a catastrophe – birds can fly from the flames, and other animals can shelter underground, or in water. However, animals such as snakes, sloths or insects, will be out-run by the flames and die.

Scarlet macaw
The biggest problems for birds are the loss of a food supply, and the danger to chicks in the nest. Scarlet macaws nest in tree-holes, so their young may suffer heat-stroke or suffocation.

Jaguar
Jaguars are so wary of man that it is very unlikely that any would stay in an area about to be cleared. If one was forced to leave by fire, it would be able to run fast enough to escape the flames, but would probably have to fight for new territory with other jaguars.

Termites
The main heat of the fire is at tree-level, so by retreating into their underground nest, termites can survive. Their nests have a series of galleries.

Fire in the forest

FIRE IS ALSO man's way of clearing the forest. Peasant farmers use 'slash-and-burn' to clear land for crops. In August 1987 there were 6803 fires in just one Brazilian province. These fires aren't natural – often escaping animals will run into another wall of flame from another fire, and perish.

The fires are a fast way of clearing the undergrowth, and the ash is rich in minerals which improve the soil for crops. But the seeds lying dormant in the soil aren't affected by fire, and soon the forest plants will start growing up among the crops. Within a year or two the soil is exhausted and the forest becomes useless scrub.

Rare monkeys

IN FEBRUARY 1990 a fire destroyed over 40 per cent of the Poco das Antas reserve near Rio de Janeiro, which is home for one of the world's rarest monkeys, the golden lion tamarin. Since 1983 there has been a scheme to increase the wild population there by releasing animals born in captivity in Europe and the United States. Over 70 monkeys have been released, and now the wild population is about 400, including some being radio-tracked by scientists.

This fire raised the questions of how to protect reserves, and whether the reserve is large enough, if nearly half can be destroyed by one fire.

The golden lion tamarin is a test-case for the survival of the whole forest. Keeping the wild population going will take a lot of money and human effort. It would have been easier to solve the tamarins' problems before they faced extinction!

Spider monkeys
Spider monkeys live in small groups, high in the trees. They use their prehensile tail to hang from branches when reaching for food, and are active enough to avoid the fire.

Butterflies
Most butterflies are not fast enough to fly in front of the flames, and unless the fire blows over them, they are unlikely to survive.

Caiman
Rivers are natural fire-breaks, so caimans and turtles should be safe from the fire if they take to the water.

Sloth
Sloths are renowned as slow movers, but they can move along branches quickly if threatened. Even so, it would be hard for a sloth to out-run a fire.

Anaconda
For snakes, the only safety is in the water or underground. A large anaconda would probably only be safe in the water. This applies to lizards too.

WILDSIDE WATCH

There is an annual burning in the Amazon in September.
● How much news coverage is there? Did you know it happens?
● The tamarins' story shows that protecting animals is best done before they have reached the verge of extinction!
● You can help the golden lion tamarin project through Marwell and Jersey Zoos. Captive-breeding schemes are a good idea but getting the animals back where they belong is difficult and expensive, so the zoos need your support.

Using the forest

THE RAINFOREST is a natural environment, with fruit, vegetables and animals providing a rich food supply for all its inhabitants, including man. In addition there are metal ores, timber, rattan, rubber and medicinal plants which are only used by man.

There is no reason why the rainforest should not be used, provided this does not mean wholesale destruction that prevents the forest from regenerating. Sensible harvesting can only be done on a small scale by people who understand the forest, not by landless peasants forced into forest areas, or by multinational companies whose only consideration is profit.

Forest people

MAN HAS LIVED in the forest for thousands of years. Places like the Amazon are home both to Indian tribes and white settlers called *caboclos*, who live within the forest without destroying it. These peoples are under threat too – the Yanomami in Brazil, Penan and Dyak in Sarawak, and others.

The Indians use between 50 and 70 per cent of the trees for some purpose, and the economics of this lifestyle are very interesting. It has been calculated that the wild crops in Peruvian jungle are worth £4300 per hectare. If it's cleared for ranching, it's worth only half as much.

Forest people live in small groups, often near a river or in a small clearing. They harvest the forest animals and plants, without causing damage. These Yanomami boys even have tame marsupial rats.

The outsiders

REGARDING the rainforest simply as an easily available source of billions of dollars' worth of timber could ultimately destroy mankind. For the forest has a far more important role in protecting man from himself, via medicinal drugs, food and the global air conditioning that reduces the greenhouse effect.

Exploitation comes in two forms: from landless peasant farmers trying to make a living in Brazil and Africa; and from industrial harvesting – again in Brazil and in Asia. Both could be better managed by involving, not excluding, the forest people. As long as demand comes from the industrial countries of the West, there will be people in the rainforest countries ready to sell off their finest asset.

Planting manioc, one of the standard food-crops for the people farming cleared forest. They will also have to grow cash-crops like coffee to buy meat and other things that they cannot grow. Their crops may only grow for a few years, then the soil is useless.

The scientists

IF WE ARE to use the rainforest sensitively, we have to know what lives there, so scientific exploration is vital. The scientists have to build walkways high in the canopy to get close enough to the animals even to see and name them. Every study finds species new to science.

Plants can be useful to man especially as a source of medicines. Rainforest plants have to protect themselves against the hordes of insects, so they produce toxic chemicals, which form the basis of many of our drugs. Some plants rely on animals to spread seeds so they produce fruits attractive to the animals and to us.

These are the biological stories behind sensible, natural use of the rainforest, but the time to discover them is limited.

Left: Scientists now use rock-climbing technology, including climbing irons and harnesses, to get close to the plants and animals high in the canopy. These studies have shown the huge range of forest wildlife.

WILDSIDE WATCH

- The Kuna Indians of Panama have created their own forest park. It protects their land and raises money from tourism, under their control.
- Among the rainforest Indians, the Waimiri Atroari of the Balbina Dam area numbered 6000 in 1900, 571 in 1982 and just 374 in 1990. They are endangered humans! They need help and protection too.
- We in the West are responsible for much of the destruction: shouldn't we pay more for rainforest products, and use the profits to protect the forest?

Green deserts

WHAT HAPPENS once the rainforest has been cleared? The peasant farmers plant their crops, which include yams and vegetables to feed themselves, and coffee or other crops to sell. The enormous variety of plants and animals has disappeared and big plantations will simply replace the huge range of forest plants with one – probably coffee – that earns money. The ashes of the burned forest improve the poor soil for the first crop but soon the forest plants will start to reinvade the land.

The coffee plantation

MAN DEVELOPED agriculture – the selective growing of food plants – thousands of years ago. It's an unnatural process, a 'monoculture' with one type of plant replacing a variety. In most countries animals can adapt, but many rainforest animals need specific plants to live.

Many of the crops are rainforest plants – coffee came originally from a bush in Ethiopia, cocoa from West Amazonia – but the original stocks are now only of use for building up the commercial strains. A plantation coffee plant is no good for a butterfly unless its caterpillars naturally feed on the wild plant. If they do, the farmer may use pesticides on it, including many now banned in the West. So the new crops draw the goodness from the soil, the chemicals poison the land and after a few years, it becomes a desert.

Plants as medicines

TWENTY PER CENT of all drugs contain extracts of rainforest plants, many of them used by local people in a raw state, yet only one per cent of rainforest plants has been examined for use in the cosmetic or drug industries.

Forest vines produce the muscle relaxant curare, cocaine comes from leaves and the malaria drug quinine comes from tree bark. Extracts from the Madagascar rosy periwinkle (now extinct in the wild) help many more children recover from leukaemia than previously. Finding out more about rainforest plants and their use to us will help to save the forest from destruction.

The rosy periwinkle, a tiny rainforest plant, produces minute quantities of a chemical which is used to treat the blood disease leukaemia.

Crop-spraying
Any survivors that can eat the crops are now pests, reducing profits. Insecticide sprays will kill the new pests, but may poison any animals that feed on the pests. The poisons may also enter the water supply.

Butterfly
The surviving animals like this butterfly may try to exploit the new single-species forest, but unless they can find nectar plants to feed on and their caterpillars can eat these leaves, they will die out. The forest animals and plants rely on each other, so changing the plants must affect the animals too.

WILDSIDE WATCH

Rainforests can be economically valuable and harvestable.
● Not all governments agree – Zaire officially regards its forests as 'of little economic value' – wasteland!
● Now the Jamaican government is planting coffee in the rainforest to try to earn money from exports.
● In Thailand they are clearing rainforest to grow cabbage and even strawberry cash-crops. And in keeping the pests down, Thailand has become the biggest importer of pesticides in South-East Asia.

Eating the rainforest

YOU MAY BE eating the rainforest! Think about it when you bite into a hamburger or a piece of tropical fruit.

Much of the forest of Central and South America has been destroyed for cattle ranching, to provide cheap beef for export. Often the ranchers come in after the first settlers' crops have failed. They have about seven years to make a profit until the poor soils stop supporting the grass and weeds make the pasture useless.

There is an alternative: as storage and international transport become easier, harvesting the forest for natural products such as fruit and nuts becomes easier too. Forest products are now more marketable, and the forest people can earn money without causing destruction.

Fruit and nuts

BANANAS, pineapples, Brazil and cashew nuts have always come from the rainforest. Now mangoes, star-fruit, lychees and other exotic fruits naturally harvested from the forest can be found in many supermarkets. Palm oil and andiroba oil can also be extracted without deforestation, since the trees these oils come from occur as natural clumps of hundreds of trees within the forest.

There is a vast untapped resource in these natural crops. In Papua New Guinea the local people gather over 200 different plants from the forest, only two of which are eaten in the West. Perhaps we should make more use of all this variety, like the animals who live in the forest.

Pineapples, mangoes, bananas, lychees, Brazil nuts and cashews are just some of the foods we enjoy that come from rainforest areas.

The hamburger connection

HUMANS eat 140 million tonnes of meat a year, with the West taking 60 per cent of this, despite having only a third of the population of the Third World. With beef consumption in Central America actually falling, meat from rainforest cattle ranches goes for export, but the huge hamburger companies deny having an effect on the rainforests.

The only exception was Burger King, which did import meat from Costa Rica, but does so no longer. They recently spent over £11 million on advertising their new-found greenness, almost 20 times the budget for Costa Rica's forest department!

In Brazil, cattle ranching creates power for the rancher, so some ranches are very big businesses. This makes the forest a pawn in a complex money game, and changing the rules won't be easy.

Top: Cattle are completely out of place in the forest, but the land laws encourage ranching, and when things start going wrong, the cattle can be quickly slaughtered for a large profit.
Left: In Europe, the beef in hamburgers comes almost entirely from European sources so it is not directly contributing to the destruction of rainforest.

WILDSIDE WATCH

● The beef in your hamburger may not come from a rainforest, but do you really need it? For a third of the world's population, there's more meat in your burger than they eat in a week.
● If there are exotic foods in your supermarket, where did they come from? Are they a crop grown on cleared land, or naturally harvested? Can anyone in the shop tell you?
● Try a new ice-cream called Rainforest Crunch, made using *harvested* nuts from the rainforest. Does it taste good?

Gone for ever?

RAINFOREST IS A complex natural system, and death for plants and animals is very common, but in nature the extinction of a whole species is rare, and takes thousands of years. The arrival of modern man and the destruction of the forest has put enormous pressure on some animals, many of which have no natural enemies.

Destruction takes many forms – tree-felling, road-building, slash-and-burn, damming of rivers and trade in animals and plants. The plants may be cut down, burned or trampled, and animals may lose their food supply or be trapped or poisoned. Human greed is causing other animals to die out and extinction is now common in the rainforest, affecting some spectacular species.

LOCATION
Central and South America
THREATENED SPECIES
Jaguar
TOTAL POPULATION
Unknown but small
THREATS
Illegal skin trade and destruction of habitat

Jaguars are fully protected by CITES (see page 19), but there is still illegal trade in their skins. These are the top carnivores of the forest - secretive and perfectly adapted for jungle life. It is impossible to know how many there are in the wild, but forest destruction is reducing the areas in which they can live, so their numbers are certain to fall.

LOCATION
Thailand
THREATENED SPECIES
Gurney's pitta
TOTAL POPULATION
31 pairs, possibly more
THREATS
Habitat destruction

Now for the good news! The Gurney's pitta or jewel thrush is a bright black-and-gold bird that lives in the forests of Thailand. There had been no trace of the species since 1952 and it was thought to be extinct until 1986, when a nest was discovered. Extensive surveys of the area revealed a further 30 pairs of pittas. The Thai government has banned logging in its forests, and enforced protection of these areas, so at least one extinction may have been halted at the very last moment.

LOCATION
Sumatra
THREATENED SPECIES
Rafflesia arnoldii
TOTAL POPULATION
Very small
THREATS
Destruction of habitat through logging

The rafflesia is the largest flower in the world and is among the most endangered. It produces a smell like rotting meat to attract the flies it uses for pollination. Logging has reduced the areas of rainforest where it is found, but in Sabah on the island of Borneo it now has legal protection.

LOCATION
Brazil
THREATENED SPECIES
Spix's macaw
TOTAL POPULATION
17 in captivity (in 1990) plus one in Brazil
THREATS
Pet trade

Spix's macaw was thought to be extinct in the wild, until a single bird was discovered in Bahia state in Brazil. It has to be protected against being stolen and sold, as its rarity increases its value. The macaws in captivity are kept behind locked doors and they are very unlikely to breed, so as the species slides towards extinction, each bird becomes more and more valuable.

WILDSIDE WATCH

There are three pressures on rainforest animals – logging, development for dams etc. and invasion by peasant farmers.
● Asia suffers most from logging, Amazonia from development and Africa from peasants.
● Extinction is final. Species can still exist in captivity, such as the Spix's macaw seems doomed to, but that is a pathetic state.
● Reintroduction from captivity isn't easy. Why did the wild population fall? Has the problem gone away? If not, the animals are being released to die.

Save the rainforest!

RAINFOREST ANIMALS and plants need your protection, but the problem goes far beyond simply caring for wildlife. The destruction comes from Western industry and from the need to earn money by poor, over-populated rainforest countries. Some, such as Costa Rica and Ecuador, are able to reduce their debt to the West in exchange for protection of the rainforest. But the exploitation continues, and there are two approaches to slowing it down: by local people and by you and me.

We are consumers of rainforest products and we can decide whether to go on using them or not. Think about the way you live, what you spend money on, what you are trying to protect, how close you are to wildlife. Think about how important the rainforests are, not just for the animals, plants and people who live there, but for all of us. Take action – you can play your own small part in helping to change the world.

The people who live in rainforest areas are now trying to prevent any more destruction. This blockade of a logging road was in Limbang, Sarawak, in 1989.

Carnival time in Rio: a float highlighting destruction of the Brazilian rainforest moves down the road.

Animal masks for impact! In Germany people have been campaigning against international banks which fund hydro-electric schemes in South America, flooding and destroying the forest.

Useful addresses

There are many organisations you can join or contact. It's a good idea to send a stamped, self-addressed envelope when you ask for information.

Environmental Investigation Agency (EIA)
208-9 Upper Street, London N1 1RL
Investigates animal problems worldwide, and is campaigning against the parrot trade.

Flora and Fauna Preservation Society
79-83 North Street
Brighton, Sussex BN1 1ZA
Operates research projects and protection schemes for many animals around the world.

Friends of the Earth
26-28 Underwood Street, London N1 7QJ
Campaigns internationally to protect the environment. They have a major scheme to reduce agricultural destruction in Ghana. Publishes the Good Wood Guide.

The Hawk Trust
Bird-of-Prey Section
London Zoo, London NW1 4RY
Helps to protect the Philippine eagle.

International Council for Bird Preservation (ICBP)
32 Cambridge Road
Girton, Cambridge CB3 0PJ
Specialist organisation protecting birds worldwide.

Jersey Wildlife Preservation Trust
Les Augres Manor
Trinity, Jersey, Channel Islands
Is taking part in a re-introduction scheme for golden lion tamarins coordinated by the National Zoo, Washington, USA.

LYNX
P.O. Box 509, Dunmow, Essex CM6 1UH
Campaigns against the fur trade.

Media Natura
45 Shelton Street, London WC2H 9HJ
Information centre, including schemes for harvesting the forests rather than destroying them.

Programme for Belize
Old Mission Hall
Sibton Green, Saxmundham, Suffolk
Raises money to protect the forests of Belize, a former British colony, with direct contacts with local people. Projects include 'selling' areas of rainforest to prevent their logging.

The Rainforest Foundation
5 Fitzroy Lodge
The Grove, London N6 5JU
Specialist organisation for the rainforest and its original human inhabitants.

Rio Mazan Project
38-40 Exchange Street, Norwich NR2 1AX
Raises funds to support the local people of Ecuador in protecting their own lands.

Royal Society for the Protection of Birds (RSPB)
The Lodge, Sandy, Bedfordshire
Mainly UK-based, but with some international projects.

Survival International
310 Edgware Road, London W2 1DY
Campaigns to protect the people who live in the rainforests, and increase their say in what happens to it. They have a special fund for Sarawak.

Worldwide Fund for Nature UK (WWF)
Panda House
Weyside Park, Godalming, Surrey GU7 1XR
International pressure group that funds schemes all over the world, including major projects on orang-utans and Madagascar.

Index

Africa 5, 6, 7, 8, 9, 16, 24, 29, 35, 48, 49, 56, 61
Alligators 20-1
Amazonia 6, 8, 9, 14-15, 18, 24, 26, 40, 41, 43, 44, 54, 56, 61
America 12, 27, 29 see also Central America, South America, United States
Anacondas 20-1, 42, 43, 46, 53
Ant-eaters 7, 10
Ants 10, 11, 14-15, 16, 34, 46
Apes 30-3
Asia 5, 6, 9, 13, 29, 32, 35, 36, 41, 43, 48, 55, 58, 61 see also South-East Asia
Australia 6, 38-9, 48

Bananas 5, 9, 58
Bark 26, 31, 49, 56
Bats 14-15, 49
Beetles 40, 46
Birds 4, 10, 14, 15, 22, 23, 24-5, 28, 34, 35, 39, 40, 41, 42, 43, 50, 52, 60
Boa constrictors 21
Brazil 6, 7, 8, 9, 21, 23, 25, 29, 36, 42, 53, 55, 59, 61, 63
Breeding 10, 14-15, 23, 25, 27, 28, 29, 31, 33, 43, 44, 50, 51, 53
Britain 8, 23, 25, 26, 36
Bush-babies 48, 49, 50
Butterflies 4, 21, 26-7, 28, 39, 46, 47, 51, 53, 56, 57

Caimans 21, 53
Camouflage 21, 22, 46, 47
Canopy 10, 16, 17, 18, 32, 39, 42, 50, 55
Captivity 24-5, 29, 31, 51, 53, 61
Capybaras 44
Cassowaries 39
Caterpillars 15, 16, 26, 27, 28, 47, 56, 57
Cat family 22-3, 44, 46, 52
Cattle ranching 5, 58-9
Central America 6, 7, 8, 9, 18, 24, 26, 55, 57, 58-9, 60-1, 62
Cheetahs 22
Chemicals 28, 55, 56
Chlorofluorocarbons (CFCs) 12
Chlorophyll 12, 16
Chocolate 9
Climate 6, 9, 12-13, 55
Cocoa 5, 8, 9, 56
Coffee 5, 8, 9, 37, 55, 56, 57
Conservation 54, 58-63 see also energy, legislation, pollution and Wildside Watch boxes on 4, 5, 7, 9, 10 and all odd-numbered pages thereafter
Crabs 34, 35
Crocodiles 20-1, 53
Crops 5, 7, 8, 9, 37, 48, 53, 55, 56, 57, 58, 59

Dams 38, 42-3, 44, 45
Deserts 8, 9, 56
Disease 9, 28, 29, 41, 56
Droughts 13

Eagles 10, 11, 24, 50-1
Ecological balance 12, 13, 35
Ecosystem 46-7
Eggs 10, 21, 27, 31, 43, 50, 51
Electricity 12, 13, 38, 42, 43
Endangered species 19, 20-1, 22-3, 24, 25, 27, 29, 36-7, 44-5, 48, 50-1, 53, 60-1
Energy 10, 12-13, 38, 42
Europe 7, 8, 12, 20, 24, 25, 27, 39, 41, 43, 53, 59
Extinction see endangered species

Farming 5, 7, 35, 37, 49, 51, 56
Fires 13, 35, 48, 52-3, 56
Fish 21, 22, 34-5, 40-1, 42, 44
Floods 13, 35, 37, 38, 40, 42-3, 45
Flowers 10, 14, 16, 26, 47, 61
Food supply see crops, habitats
Forest floor 10, 26
Fossil fuels 7, 12, 13, 35
Frogs 4, 10, 21, 34, 36, 46, 47
Fruit 4, 7, 9, 14-15, 24, 31, 33, 39, 48, 49, 55, 58
Fur and skin trade 20-1, 22-3, 60

Gases 12-13
Gibbons 32-3
Greenhouse effect 12-13, 55
Growth cycles 12-13, 16-17

Habitats, destruction of 16-17, 27, 32-3, 50, 60-1
Hamburgers 58, 59
Hardwood 5, 8, 16, 32
Harvesting, natural 54, 58-9
Hunting 20-3, 50

Indians 54, 55
Industry 6, 7, 15, 32, 56, 62
Insects 4, 10, 14, 15, 16, 18, 19, 21, 26-7, 28, 31, 33, 34, 40, 46-7, 48, 49, 52, 53, 55

Jaguars 22, 23, 44, 46, 52

Kangaroos 39
Kingfishers 41

Leather trade 20-1, 45
Leaves 10, 12-13, 15, 16, 18, 21, 31
Legislation 22, 23, 24, 25, 41, 44, 60-1
Lemurs 32, 36-7, 48, 50
Leopards 22
Lizards 21

Macaws 11, 16, 24, 25, 52, 61
Mammals 4, 10, 14, 15, 21, 22-3, 28, 29, 36, 44-5, 51
Man 7, 50, 51, 53, 54, 56, 60
Mangrove swamps 34-5
Margays 22, 23
Medicinal plants 29, 54, 55, 56
Mining 38, 40, 41, 44, 54
Monkeys 10, 16, 32, 34, 36, 42, 48, 50, 52, 53
Mosses 18, 46
Mudskippers 35

Nectar 4, 14-15, 26, 28, 39, 57
Nests 31, 43, 51
Nuts 7, 8, 31, 58, 59

Ocelots 22
Oils 8, 12, 58
Orang-utans 30-1, 46
Orchids 11, 18, 19
Otters 44-5
Overpopulation 5, 6, 7, 35, 49, 62
Oxygen 12-13, 34

Palms 19, 27, 46, 58
Parrots 24, 25, 39, 61
Pests 29, 34, 45, 56, 57
Pet trade 20, 24-5, 31, 61
Photosynthesis 12-13, 18
Piranhas 41
Plantations 7, 8, 27, 56
Plants see greenhouse effect, growth cycles, pollination, trade
Poison 29, 40, 41, 57, 60
Pollination 14-15, 26, 28, 61
Pollution 9, 12-13, 40-1, 44, 45, 56, 57
Possums 39
Prehistoric forests 6
Primates 16, 30-7, 48-9, 50
Pythons 20-1, 47

Rain 6, 18, 37, 40-1
Rainforest layers 10-11
Reptiles 20-1, 23, 36, 47, 53
Rhinoceroses 28-9

Riverbanks and rivers 7, 20-1, 28, 29, 40, 42-3, 44-5, 54
Roads 32, 33, 38
Roots 12, 16, 18, 34

Saplings 10, 15, 30
Sea 13, 34-5
Seeds 14-15, 16, 24, 40, 53, 55
Shellfish 34, 35
Slash-and-burn 35, 48, 52
Sloths 52-3
Snakes 10, 20-1, 40, 42, 43, 47, 52-3
Soil 5, 10, 16, 28, 37, 43, 53, 55, 58
South America 6, 7, 8, 9, 10, 19, 20, 21, 24, 35, 41, 44, 45, 54, 58-9, 60-1, 62 see also Amazonia, Brazil
South-East Asia 4, 5, 6, 7, 9, 10, 19, 24, 26-35, 38, 43, 45, 50, 51, 57, 58, 60, 61, 63
Stick-insects 10, 11, 46
Sugar cane 7, 8, 9, 28, 38
Sunlight 10-11, 12-13, 16, 18

Tapirs 44-5
Temperature 6, 12-13
Termites 10, 46, 52
Threats to rainforests see dams, hunting, roads, slash-and-burn, trade
Timber see trade
Toucans 11
Trade
  cash crops 5, 7, 8, 9, 37, 48, 53, 55, 56, 57
  furs and skins 20-1, 22-3, 44, 60
  timber 5, 8, 9, 14, 15, 16-17, 19, 26, 28, 30, 32-3, 38, 41, 43, 48, 51, 54, 55, 60-1, 63
  tropical plants and animals 19, 24-5, 31
Trees see bark, greenhouse effect, growth cycles, oils, roots, trade, timber
Turtles 40-1, 42, 43, 53

Understorey 10, 18, 30, 39
United States 8, 13, 24, 25, 26, 53

Vines 10, 17, 18, 27, 30, 39

Water see dams, floods, pollution, rain, riverbanks and rivers, sea
Western world 7, 55, 56, 58, 59, 62
Wood see trade, timber

Zoos 29, 30, 31, 53

Picture credits (key: l – left, r – right, t – top, c – centre, b – bottom, tl – top left, tr – top right, bl – bottom left, br – bottom right)
Ardea pages 4 (br, F. Gohier), 6 (A. Hayward), 20 (l, J. Mason), 29 (P. Morris), 36 (b, A. Warren), 38 (tr, H. & J. Beste), 44 (b, A. Warren), 44-5 (t, K. & L. Laidler) & 60 (r, K. W. Fink); **Karen Bishop** page 30; **British Museum, Natural History** page 27 (b); **Bruce Coleman** pages 4 (bl, G. Cubitt), 18 (P. Ward), 26-7 (C. & D. Frith), 28-9 (b, L. C. Marigo), 38 (tl, F. Prenzel), 53 (R. Williams), 56 (O. Langrand) & 61 (l, A. Compost); **Susan Cunningham** page 63 (t); **Nigel Dickinson** page 62; **Mark Edwards/Still Pictures** pages 5 (br) and 17; **Environmental Investigation Agency** page 25 (r); **Environmental Picture Library** page 5 (bl, N. Dickinson); **Michael Fogden** page 47 (c); **Robin Hanbury-Tenison** page 7 (t); **Robert Harding** pages 4 (t), 5 (c, C. Bryan) & 54 (R. Hanbury-Tenison); **Eric & David Hosking** page 37 (t); **Hulton-Deutsch Collection** pages 7 (b) and 8; **Frank Lane** pages 28-9 (t), 31 & 60 (l, Silvestris); **Magnum** (M. Nichols) pages 54-5 & 58-9; **Luiz Claudio Marigo** pages 22, 22-3, 47 (t), 55 & 61 (r); **NHPA** pages 4 (c, J. Sauvanet), 20-21 (M. Wendler), 21 (b, M. Wendler), 23 (both, M. Wendler), 24, (l, J. Sauvanet), 27 (t, D. Dickins), 37 (b, M. Wendler), 38-9 (ANT/Ted Mead), 39 (R. Mackay) & 46-7 (G. Bernard); **Oxford Scientific Films** pages 5 (t, P. Devries), 16-17 (M. Pidgeon), 20 (r, K. Sandved) & 44-5 (b, Partridge Films); **Planet Earth Pictures** pages 6-7, 8-9, 36 (t, P. Chapman), **Paul Popper** page 9 (t); **Rettet den Regenwald** page 63 (b); **Royal Commonwealth Society** page 9 (c & b); **Survival Anglia** page 47 (b). BBC photographs pages 18-19, 24 (t & br), 25 (l) & 58 by Martin Norris.
Illustrators Stephen Lings, Alan Male, Shane Marsh, David Moore, Jane Pickering, Sebastian Quigley, Phil Weare, David Webb, (Linden Artists). Richard Phipps, Helen Senior.